HORSES FOR COURSES

BELFAST

*Down Royal

Downpatrick*

*Sligo

Dundalk*

*Ballinrobe   *Roscommon   *Navan   *Laytown
                                                     *Bellewstown
*Galway   *Kilbeggan   *Fairyhouse

                                        DUBLIN
                                        *Leopardstown
                            *Naas   *Punchestown
                          *The Curragh

              *Thurles
*Limerick   *Gowran Park
*Listowel
              *Tipperary
*Tralee
              *Clonmel   *Wexford
*Killarney *Cork (Mallow)
                      *Tramore
        ● CORK

                        Cheltenham
                        01242 513014

BALLINROBE	094 9541811
BELLEWSTOWN	041 9842111
CLONMEL	052 72481
CORK (Marrow)	022 50207
THE CURRAGH	045 441205
DOWNPATRICK	44612054
DOWN ROYAL	92621256
DUNDALK	042 9334438
FAIRYHOUSE	01 8256167
GALWAY	091 753870
GOWRAN PARK	056 7726225
LEOPARDSTOWN	01 2890500
LIMERICK	061 320000
LISTOWEL	068 21144
KILLARNEY	064 31125
NAAS	045 897391
NAVAN	046 9021350
PUNCHESTOWN	045 897704
SLIGO	071 9183342
THURLES	0504 22253
TIPPERARY	062 51357
TRALEE	066 7126188
TRAMORE	051 381425
WEXFORD	053 43412

Anne Holland

HORSES FOR COURSES

An Irish Racing Year

MAINSTREAM
PUBLISHING
EDINBURGH AND LONDON

First published in Great Britain in 2005 by
MAINSTREAM PUBLISHING COMPANY (EDINBURGH) LTD
7 Albany Street
Edinburgh EH1 3UG

ISBN 1 84018 910 X

A catalogue record for this book is available from the British Library

Typeset in Garamond and Gill
Printed and bound in Germany by Appl

ACKNOWLEDGEMENTS

Without the help of a great many people who gave their time freely, answered my questions patiently and told their stories generously, it would have been impossible to write this book. Every racecourse has helped, as well as individuals who have recounted their tales; the result is a range of characters and occasions (the tip of the iceberg, really) which illustrate a typical year's racing in Ireland.

To everyone who has helped, I give a huge thank you (in alphabetical order): Evan Arkwright, Sean Bell, Enda Bolger, Martin Brassil, James Burns, Margaret Byrne, Kevin Coleman, Sarah Collen, Joe Connelly, Tom Cooper, Frances Crowley, Jim Culloty, Brendan Daly, Jerry Desmond, Mannix Dowdall, Jim Dreaper, Iain Duff, Paddy Dunican, Michael Finneran, Brian Fitzsimmons, John Flannelly, Shane Fleming, Tom Gallagher, Richie Galway, Paddy Graffin, Timothy Griffin, Jessica Harrington, Louise Harrison, Sophie Hayley, Horse Racing Ireland, Michael Hourigan, Angus Houston, Dessie Hughes, *Irish Field*, Irish National Stud, Ted Kelly, Brian Kennedy, Tom and Peg Lacy, Michael Lane, Eamon Leigh, Hugh Leonard, Gail List, John Looney, Richard Lyttle, Margaret McGuinness, J.P. McManus, Peter McNiele, John Moloney, Jimmy Mangan, Jim Martin, Martinstown Stud, Noel Meade, Pierce Molony, Arthur Moore, Gearoid Moyningham, Paddy and Maureen Mullins, William Mullins,

Michael Murphy, Colm Murray, Derek Nally, Gillian O'Brien, Matt O'Dwyer, Michael O'Rourke, Dick O'Sullivan, Sue Phelan, Cecily Purcell, *Racing Post*, Peter Roe, Dick Sheil, Pat Smullen, Michael Smurfit, Paul Stephenson, Tom Taaffe, Michael Todd, Ruby Walsh, Dermot Weld, Jane Williams, and Zoe (for looking after things at home on the frequent occasions that I was away on research). I am indebted to Martin Murphy of Horse Racing Ireland for his meticulous scrutiny of the manuscript and to Deborah Warner from Mainstream for her painstaking editing (come racing soon, Debs.)

Pictures by Garr Photography, except: Bright Trick loaned by Brian Fitzsimmons, Tramore loaned by Sue Phelan, the Big Double, Punchestown, by the late Margaret Holland, the new stand Dundalk loaned by Dundalk, Urban Sea loaned by the Irish National Stud and Arkle by the author.

CONTENTS

INTRODUCTION

Visiting every Irish racecourse and meeting many of Ireland's racing personalities – horses as well as humans – has, of course, been pure pleasure. Every single course has its own special qualities and atmosphere, but there are two things common to all: a warm welcome and good sport.

The people and horses featured within these pages are examples of the whole broad brush of characters that make up Irish racing past and present, and I only wish there was room to fit in more – old and current, horses and humans, alike.

The diversity of Irish courses is huge. Scenic Sligo is set in 56 acres, Limerick's Greenmount Park in 280. They also bring a whole new meaning to the word hill.

When the Irish refer to a hill, they don't mean a gentle slope; witness Tramore and Downpatrick. And the Irish, to their credit, are not afraid to run on heavy (quite possibly bottomless) ground; not for them does heavy mean the soft side of good . . .

Ireland (and the UK) can truly boast variety, and this sets them apart from countries around the world where – dare one say it – the tracks are boring, the type and format being the same throughout, right down to all going in the same direction. Bad luck on a horse that likes to go the other way round, or who might relish the challenge of a hill, or of nipping around twists and turns.

Nearly every Irish course has at least one

race named after an old favourite racehorse, too, keeping their memories alive. Horses for courses. That's what Irish racing is all about. And the craic, of course.

What is so apparent at the country courses is the huge level of support from the local population. It may be raining (will quite likely be, for that matter) and the races may be 'ordinary', but the stands will still be crowded, especially at the various evening meetings during summer. This is their sport; their evening out; their chance for a beer, a bet and good company. Much has been done to improve racecourse facilities since the mid-1990s, and there is huge ongoing investment. The Curragh will be a state-of-the-art course by 2008, and before long there will be an all-weather course at Dundalk.

I am in the fortunate position of living between Kilbeggan, Ireland's only all-NH (National Hunt) course, and The Curragh, the only turf all-flat course and home to all five Irish Classics, so I couldn't be better placed for sampling the isle's wide diversity of meetings. I have enjoyed visiting them all, without exception, and I believe this shines through in the following pages. It will surprise some readers, but when I visited Clonmel, my reaction was to reach out for my long-since hung-up boots; I could just imagine sweeping down that hill and then heading for home, a good horse beneath me . . .

As a child in England I always knew my parents would be away for a few days in late April or early May and again in July, for which read Punchestown and Killarney, so both meetings hold sentimental value.

There are little differences between England and Ireland, nuances almost. In Ireland, for instance, the first half-dozen or more horses past the post are announced in the official results. In England it's the first four. And I have yet to understand why an 'open ditch' (Great Britain) is a 'regulation' in Ireland, yet it has been ever thus. When a jockey has drawn his correct weight after passing the post first, the English announcement is 'weighed in'; in Ireland it is the evocative 'winner all right' – either way, it means successful punters can go and collect their winnings. Ireland will have up to three reserve horses declared for many races, allowing one or more to have a run should a horse or two in the main list be unable; but, unlike England, there are no selling races (when the winner of such a race is put up for auction immediately afterwards). There is the Irish practice of running 'schooling bumpers' that are full-blown races in all but name, giving a newcomer valuable racecourse experience without running the risk of being arraigned for 'schooling in public'. Another difference is that there is much more mixing and matching between hurdling, chasing and running on the Flat here. The majority of cards are mixed meetings, though one or two Irish NH meetings have no steeplechases. In England a horse will either be a hurdler, or a steeplechaser, or a flat racer, with only occasional exceptions. But it means the Irish produce versatile horses – and it is a practice that can prove useful by preserving the handicap rating in a particular discipline until wanted for a specific important race.

And although Ireland increased its number of meetings from 305 to 313 in 2005, this still means there isn't racing every day. Yet with 27 courses it has far more than Great Britain per square mile, all of them well supported. But then racing is part of the Irish culture, part of its way of life; at Thurles it is part of family life, it being the only family-owned and run course. Many meetings have a Ladies Day, with a substantial prize for the best-dressed lady. The same official faces keep popping up, too: someone who is, say, a starter at a southern meeting may also be the judge at a track in the west and, for good measure, the clerk of the course in, perhaps, the north.

Ireland loves its festivals and has many of them: Cork and Fairyhouse at Easter, the Classic festivals at The Curragh, separately for the Guineas, the Derby and the Oaks.

Bellewstown sets the summer festivals going. Indeed, summer can be one long round of them, Killarney following on next. Then it is Galway, featuring the Galway Plate, taking in a full seven days at the end of July (just before Ireland's premier horse show at the Royal Dublin Society in Ballsbridge, Dublin, in the first week of August).

Tramore by the seaside and then Tralee, with its International Rose of Tralee contest, follow hot on its heels, and in September, after the hay and the harvest is in, the farmers descend on Listowel from all over the country for its week-long festival, run with aplomb by octogenarian Brendan Daly. Gowran Park's festival is in October and in November it is the turn of Down Royal in the North.

Prestigious Christmas festivals are held by both Limerick and Leopardstown, while, finally, there is the island's premier NH festival at Punchestown in late April or early May, Ireland's own-brand answer to England's NH festival at Cheltenham. Talking of which, I make no apology for including Cheltenham in my account of an Irish racing year . . . 10,000 Irish cross the water for it and the rest of the country stops for it anyway!

Apart from the Irish National, *the* Grand National to the Irish, at Fairyhouse on Easter Monday (an annual diary entry even for many non-regular racegoers), many other tracks have their own 'national'. The Midlands National is run at Kilbeggan, the Kerry National at Listowel, the Munster National at Limerick, the Ulster National at Downpatrick and Cork's own national – all of these keep the excitement and magic of racing in the public eye.

Miles of golden sand at Laytown . . . hooves pounding like drumbeats

National Hunt star or Derby prospect can can be seen in action. A future Gold Cup winner might also be seen at a point-to-point (Best Mate is not the only example). And there is pony racing, a branch of racing integral to Ireland, which is usually fiercely contested around muddy fields or on sandy beaches where the mounts are ridden by boys (and girls) many of whom go on to make their name in the 'grown-up' sport.

There has simply not been room to include point-to-pointing and pony racing within these pages other than in passing, but they, too, are part of the culture and heritage of racing in Ireland. Another time, perhaps.

The major flat races, by contrast, are shared by just two courses: ten of them at The Curragh and two, including the Champion Stakes, at Leopardstown.

And then there is Laytown. Well, simply read on . . .

There can be no better way of getting to know the island of Ireland than by visiting its racecourses, from the glamour of Leopardstown and the class of The Curragh to the majestic mountains around Killarney and the unique challenge of Downpatrick, the warmth of welcome at Gowran Park and Clonmel to the summer holidaymakers' meetings and the 'industry' days in the winter months. It can be at any one of these that a potential

They're off! Pony racing on the beach at Ballyheigue, Co. Kerry, July 2005

JANUARY

GOWRAN PARK

Gowran Park is a gem, not just for its setting, which is superb, nor for its excellent modern facilities (some people remember the old stand nostalgically), but for its atmosphere and the feeling of caring, a mood that is apparent at many other courses too. There is little doubt that at Gowran this is due in great part to its directors and team players, from chairman Joe Connolly (Mr Red Mills) to its dynamic and efficient general manager, Jane Williams. Between them they ensure that every visitor is made to feel welcome and that every horse will run on a well-tended course.

I am there for the Christmas meeting, and there are many of the year's sponsors present, as well as jovial office parties, with much festive fare on offer in the warmth of the clubhouse bar and corporate suite restaurant.

Outside, as I walk the course, it is biting, not only the wind but also the 'verbals' coming from the jockeys as they sort themselves out in a big field over the first two flights on the far side of the course, well out of earshot of the stands. The back straight is gently uphill and the chase course has four inviting fences up it, bounded on the far side by fir trees, leading into an extension of the golf course. On the top bend there is a narrow opening off through the trees for the golfers, testing their skills. But now we're back to the skills of the jockeys, and as

Settling down among the verbals at Gowran Park

they round the right-handed bend and swing slightly downhill there are three fences left.

After racing, back in the warmth of the restaurant there is a brilliant band playing, an extraordinarily disparate quintet who play with such verve and *joie de vivre* that my feet start itching to dance.

Gowran Park's main race of the year is the Thyestes Chase in January, a three-mile handicap that has been won in the past by the likes of Arkle, Flyingbolt, Fort Leney and Brown Lad, all of them Dreaper-trained in the heady '60s and '70s.

The extraordinary thing about Thyestes, the horse after whom the famous steeplechase is named, is that he was a flat racehorse who only ever ran in two sprints

(which he won), and they were in England, at Sandown and Goodwood. But he was bred close to Gowran at Mount Juliet by Major Dermot McCalmont, a lifelong friend to Gowran (and to racing), who had him in training in Stockbridge, Hampshire, with Atty Persse. Thyestes, the third-rated two year old of 1930, was the son of Tetrama and grandson of The Tetrarch, and he went to stud in Yorkshire. Major McCalmont, however, presented a Thyestes trophy to the Kilkenny Show for the five-year-old hunter class. There was only one contestant, and its owner, John McEnery of Rossenarra Stud, duly won the trophy. (It was the McEnerys who bred Red Rum, but he never ran at Gowran.) In 1954 John presented the trophy to Gowran Park for the first running of the Thyestes Chase.

So, while the original winner of the trophy was an obscure hunter who had a walk over, the standard of the steeplechase winners has always been top class. The first winner was Prince of Devon, owned by Mrs Ursula Magnier, trained by Mr Clem Magnier and ridden by Mr Eddie Newman. Also in the race were Royal Tan, who fell and then won the Aintree Grand National that spring, and Carey's Cottage, who was placed at Aintree the following year.

As I write in 2005 the most recent winner is Numbersixvalverde, who gave his 12-horse Curragh-trainer Martin Brassil and amateur rider N.P. 'Slippers' Madden, aged 19, the biggest win of their

14

careers by the shortest of margins. It was one of those occasions when one wished it could be called a dead heat, for Kymandjen, who had led from flag-fall, was literally beaten 'on the nod' in an epic front-running performance. At Easter Numbersixvalverde crowned even that performance by gamely winning the Irish Grand National at Fairyhouse, Martin Brassil's first-ever runner in the race, with Ruby Walsh in the saddle.

Back at Gowran's Thyestes meeting, there is a two-and-a-half-mile handicap chase commemorating both Carey's Cottage and Ashkalani. Ashkalani never raced at Gowran Park but is standing at Coolamurray Stud, in Co. Wexford, which is sponsoring the race – during 2005 I had a splendid day's hunting on his half-brother, a brilliant jumper but so slow that he couldn't even place in a point-to-point, such are the inconsistencies of breeding!

Since its birth in 1914 (there having been racing at two localities in the district prior to then) Gowran has always been innovative. The present company was formed in 1948 and its first secretary and managing director, Jack Duggan, initiated the first Irish race meeting to be televised from here. Racing takes place throughout the year at Gowran Park and apart from the Thyestes it also hosts the Red Mills Trial Hurdle in February, an acknowledged pre-Cheltenham trial that was won in 2005 by Hardy Eustace before his triumphant second Champion Hurdle at

Cheltenham, and the Glanbia Classic Trial held in early May. Several famous horses have won on their debut here, Refuse To Bend winning as a two year old before going on to win four Group 1 races, including the 2,000 Guineas of 2003. Levmoss, who won both the Ascot Gold Cup and the Prix de l'Arc de Triomphe of 1969, also made his debut at Gowran a winning one.

Set in a historic part of Co. Kilkenny, with the Glencaughan Mountains to the east and Mount Leinster deigning to show its 2,610-ft peak on a clear day, stories of Gowran abound. It is said that in 1649 when Oliver Cromwell was invading, he stopped a tramp by the name of Annaly and asked him how he could capture the town of Gowran. The tramp pondered, then thought of the many pigeons living in the thatched roofs of the town's houses. He told Cromwell to soak wheat in whiskey and place it on the road. When the pigeons saw it, he said, they would land and eat it and become so drunk they could be easily caught. He told Cromwell to tie burning rags to their feet when they sobered up and release them, whereupon they would fly straight back to their roosts, setting fire to the thatch. Before long the town was burnt to the ground, allowing the attack to be successful due to the double confusion and victory with minimal loss to Cromwell.

To reward the tramp, it is said, Cromwell ennobled him, naming him

Lord Annaly of Gowran and making him landlord of much of the surrounding land. The current racecourse site was his lawn and he planted all the trees in patterns to resemble a suit of cards. Look at the paddock area and try to decipher which suit it once represented!

Cromwell also ransacked nearby Paulstown. To this day the land where they camped between the two towns is known as the Red Bog, due to the colour of the invading soldiers' uniforms and from the fires they lit. Nearby Bloody Bridge gets its name from the blood that was spilled during battle which flowed into the river at this point, turning its waters red.

* * *

Gowran Park chairman Joe Connolly has his roots in the area. His great-grandfather returned to the bakery business from the USA in 1866 and purchased the Red Mills at nearby Goresbridge in 1908, producing the animal feeds that succeeding Connolly generations have continued to evolve. Joe and his brother Bill are fourth generation and Joe's two sons, Garreth and William, who work in the business, represent the fifth.

Joe has been chairman of Gowran Park since 1997, when it needed to be 'modernised but not ruined'. A €6.5 million development project has meant a new grandstand, plus stables and a parade ring. An 18-hole championship golf course was also built, designed by Canadian Jeff Howes, who was responsible for the greens and tees at the world-renowned Mount Juliet, Co. Kilkenny – a real feather in Gowran's cap, as its 500 golfing members will testify. A year after taking over Gowran Park's reins Joe's father, Liam, died.

A keen point-to-point fan who rode with some success, Liam was in the same class in school as Paddy Mullins (as Joe was with Willie Mullins a generation later). It was about 1960 that Paddy had a horse that was proving a finicky feeder; Paddy went to 'the Mill' looking for suggestions. Liam tried cooking the ingredients and the horse thrived on it, going on to win several races – and so the ready-mixed cooked feed that we are familiar with today was born.

Continuity is part of the Gowran tradition, and the track foreman is Pat

Ground staff removing the hurdles prior to the bumper

Walsh, whose grandfather, father and brothers have all been associated with Gowran Park since its inception, his brothers then moving on to Royal Windsor racecourse in England. And there is Joe Bollard, a remarkable nonagenarian. He worked for Jack Duggan in his shop and also on race days, turning his hand to whatever was needed. That was from 1948, and he continued to work for successive Gowran managers until the 1990s. What's more, at the time of writing he is still active and retains a great memory.

I visit the well-stocked saddlery stand of Anne Porter. It was her uncle, Dan Kirwan, who originally owned and trained Nicolaus Silver from his Lower Grange stables near Gowran. The beautiful grey went on to win the 1961 Grand National at Aintree in the hands of Irishman Bobby Beasley. It was he who had spotted him running in Naas the previous year and thought, 'What a good-looking horse; what a pity he's so moderate.'

Nicolaus Silver was sold in Ballsbridge to Fred Rimell; Tim Brookshaw could have ridden him in the National, but he thought him too careful for Liverpool, and so Bobby Beasley came in for the winning ride. In later years Nicolaus Silver died while out hunting in Sussex.

Another great little horse around Gowran was Prince of Aragon owned by T.A. Connelly (a cousin of the Red Mills family) and trained by James J. O'Donnell

at Clashwilliam. Prince of Aragon won a three-mile hurdle and another race in Gowran, and finished second in the Thyestes; he won about sixteen races in all, usually ridden either by Johnny Gourey or the legendary T.P. Burns. James J. O'Donnell's sons, Kevin, A.S. and Joe, all won Ireland's longest race, the La Touche at Punchestown.

But the most famous local trainer of all is the incredible Paddy Mullins.

* * *

'Do you miss her?'

It is approaching 20 years since the death of Dawn Run, and with many fine achievements since, not least training a Classic winner at the age of 84, that is still the most frequently asked question of Paddy Mullins, the retiring superstar of Irish racing from Doninga, near Goresbridge, in Co. Kilkenny.

It is fair to say 'the Mare', as Dawn Run was known, was unique. She is still the only horse to have won both the Champion Hurdle and the Cheltenham Gold Cup, and in the same season in the year of her hurdle triumph she also won the French and Irish Champion Hurdles, another feat that has not been emulated.

It was on the same French soil, after her Gold Cup win two years later, that Dawn Run met her death. Nearly 20 years later, still virtually every Irishman remembers the occasion and deplores it, declaring she should not have run. Sure, people still say vehemently, and hadn't she achieved enough by winning the Gold Cup and then a special match race against her lifelong rival Buck House.

It is sad that Dawn Run is remembered for the wrong reasons, though the horse herself was admired immensely, and rightly so: she won most of her races – the first, a bumper, with her grandmother owner Charmian Hill in the saddle, two more on the level, thirteen hurdles and five chases before her career ended prematurely attempting to win the French Champion Hurdle (the Grande Course de Haies d'Auteuil), where she broke her neck.

'I always regret that I declared her that day,' Maureen Mullins says poignantly. 'She was a brilliant mare.'

The answer to the most-asked question incidentally (Do you miss her?) is, 'Of course we do, and as the years roll by we realise even more how good she was, hurdles and fences equally brilliant.'

We look at a photograph of Dawn Run in a book published immediately before her Gold Cup win, which features the whole family – Paddy, Maureen, Willie, George, Tony, Tom and Sandra. Underneath, the caption reads that every one of them had ridden a winner.

'Now, all bar George, who has gone into the equine transport business, have trained winners too,' says Maureen, justifiably proud.

The most recent to join the training ranks is Tom, who, in the summer of 2004, had trained ten winners in the first two months of holding a licence, including Liberman. Tom had got 'fed up' of waiting for his indefatigable father to retire, though he still did much to help him as well. In February 2005, the 86-year-old Paddy Mullins called time, and handed over his long-held licence to the regret and admiration of many. It turned out that the last winner he trained was the exciting mare Asian Maze, who won at Punchestown on New Year's Eve 2004, and she continued her winning ways for Tom.

Sandra, married to one of the Horse Racing Ireland directors, Peter McCarthy, is involved in the Owners Association and lives in Dungarvin, Co. Kilkenny. She won the Rose of Tralee race on her mother's home-bred I'm Ready in 1980 before the mare went on to win that year's Irish Cambridgeshire. Tony, forever remembered for his winning rides on Dawn Run, trains beside Gowran Park racecourse and has 'a brilliant new gallop'.

Willie trains at Leighlinbridge from where he sent out the wonderful Florida Pearl, retired in 2004, to his many successes. In the summer of 2004 he also sent Rule Supreme to win that same French Champion Hurdle as Dawn Run.

In April 2005, what seemed like the whole of Leighlinbridge, including many children, welcomed home Willie's Grand

them showing talent, including Daniel, one of Tony's two sons, who has won the 12.2hh Champion Show Jumping at the Dublin Show in both 2003 and 2004.

As a mother and wife, Maureen picks out each of her family's different personal highlights: the day Tony rode Grabel to win the world's richest hurdle race in Duelling Grounds, Kentucky, in April 1990. Grabel was a mare that won 24 races, 11 of them at Punchestown, where she was unbeaten. For Willie it is the day he rode as well as trained Whither Or Which to win at Cheltenham (and now Hedgehunter's National), and for George the day he won a novice chase on Luska in Clonmel before that horse went on to win the Irish National.

National hero Hedgehunter, with all the Mullins' families there. Hedgehunter, ears pricked, eyes alert, looked as fresh as a daisy, despite having run in the marathon the day before, travelled home by ferry and been paraded at Leopardstown! He posed patiently and behaved like the perfect gentleman – even when Ruby Walsh hopped up bareback on him – until darkness fell and he finally went home to his own stable, while the celebrations continued into the wee hours inside The Lord Bagnal Inn.

Then there are the Mullins grandchildren, current tally ten, all of

Children welcome home Grand National hero Hedgehunter

In the dusk, Ruby Walsh and Hedgehunter
are reunited

For Sandra it is the day she won the
Rose of Tralee and for Tom it is winning
on Dawn Run in a flat race, also at Tralee,
from a field that included no less than 15
previous winners.

Then we come to Paddy.

'I'm not going to say Dawn Run's Gold
Cup as the special moment because Mrs
Hill had taken Tony off,' Maureen
ponders, 'and so it wasn't the greatest for
me.' She thinks hard, and meanwhile
nominates Vintage Tipple as their most
memorable flat-racing success. She won
the Irish Oaks in the summer of 2003, a
reminder for all, lest any should forget,
that Paddy was also a top-class flat-race
trainer. The stupendous reception that
Paddy Mullins, more than horse or rider,

was given that day will go down forever
in the annals of The Curragh.

The story of Vintage Tipple is itself a fairy
tale. She was bought by rookie owner Pat
O'Donovan, a west Cork businessman, for
the incredibly modest sum of 16,000
guineas. 'It was something that will never
happen again,' says Maureen. 'She was
bought by an "ordinary" owner and instead
of sending her to a "proper" flat trainer he
chose Paddy because he admired him. She
won the greatest Irish race for a filly with
Frankie Dettori in the saddle; he is brilliant
and a lovely person, he's so good for racing.

'We knew before the race that she
should be there or thereabouts. The owner
had had some very tempting offers, but he
refused them all.'

We come back to her outstanding NH
memory for Paddy and she plumps for
Herring Gull, for his win in the Tote (now
Royal & SunAlliance) Novices Chase at
the Cheltenham Festival. He won the Irish
National the following month and went
on to win a prestigious French race at
Auteuil, with Stan Mellor in the saddle.

Among the last horses Paddy trained
was Hurry Bob. He won at Punchestown
and Cork and is out of the half-sister to
their best flat horse previously, Hurry
Harriet, who won the Champion Stakes at
Newmarket back in 1973, beating Allez
France. Other big flat wins have been the
Cambridgeshire with I'm Ready and the
Cesarewitch with Height Of Fashion, who
would have been considered the best mare

most trainers would ever have, had Dawn Run not come along to rewrite the records for the distaff side. Paddy also won the Lincoln Handicap with Girl In Blue the day Dawn Run won the Page 3 Hurdle at Liverpool. Another top-class filly was Bermuda Classic, also home-bred, who won two big races at The Curragh in 1985: the Railway Stakes, ridden by Brent Thompson, and two weeks later the Nishapour Curragh Stakes, ridden by Willie Carson.

But it is for National Hunt – and Dawn Run in particular – that Paddy Mullins is best remembered. In a career spanning more than fifty years, Paddy has won four Irish Grand Nationals, with Vulpine, Herring Gull, Dim Wit and Luska; the Galway Hurdle with Negrada, Prince Tammy and Pearlstone; and the Galway Plate with O'Leary, Boro Quarter (bred and owned by Dawn Run's owner Charmian Hill), The Gooser and, in 2003, with Nearly A Moose, as well as many Cheltenham winners.

There are those who remember Paddy as a leading amateur rider too, a career which included, in 1953, winning the two big banks races, the La Touche at Punchestown, still a feature of the April festival, and a similar now-defunct race at Fairyhouse. The horse he rode was Flash Parade, and Paddy loved riding across country. He and his brother Jim rode in a lot of point-to-points along with contemporary Con Power, grandfather of

current jockey Robert Power. He rode about 25 point-to-point winners, and 14 under NH Rules.

Neither must we forget Maureen's own winning ride, which was on the white-grey full horse RazzoForte in a charity race at their local track, Gowran Park, in which daughter Sandra finished third.

Until February 2005, Paddy was still training a number of horses, many of them home-bred. He checks the mares and young stock out at grass himself every day. He has trained nearly 200 home-bred winners in all – an amazing feat.

'But we currently have plentiful fillies, and even with races for mares and fillies there are still too many; if you sell them, they don't even cover the cost of the stud fee, so we have to sell the colts,' he says, reflecting a nationwide problem.

'But I have some exciting prospects to train, though Tom has many of them now,' he said, speaking shortly before his retirement. That effervescent twinkle was still in his eye. He is revered and admired throughout Ireland and at Gowran Park, where he was leading trainer countless times, he is held in special affection.

In November 2004 Paddy and Maureen Mullins celebrated their Golden Wedding Anniversary. Their home, a traditional long, low, white-painted farmhouse, is full of family memorabilia. They and their family are a wonderful tribute to Irish racing and family life.

THURLES

The only privately owned racecourse in Ireland, Thurles presents a new dimension on the term 'family run'. On any of the dozen or so winter days when racing takes place on this undulating track in Co. Tipperary, all of the six members of the Molony family are likely to undertake one or more of the race-day duties.

Pierce Molony is the general manager and his wife, Riona, has taken over the catering with a partner, producing hot food freshly prepared on the day. Their four daughters, Patricia, Helen, AnneMarie and Kate, fill any necessary role, be it manning the entrance stiles, working in the office, selling the racecards, cleaning out the toilets, acting as barmaids, or checking the post-racing schooling tickets, cleaning up the bars and clearing away the litter after racing.

They are a cheerful bunch, these young ladies, and they perform the tasks willingly. Thurles racecourse is, after all, in their blood and has been for at least four generations.

It was in 1732 that a travel paper called *Pue's Occurrences* (now in the library of Trinity College, Dublin) first noted a three-day June meeting at Thurles, but this was intermittent. It was in the 1800s, when the property and land came into the Molony family, that racing was revived. The present owner's grandfather, also Pierce Molony, and great-great-uncle Con, took over the running of the track in the early 1900s. Grandfather Pierce Molony was also senior steward of the Turf Club, as is his namesake today, a cousin of the Thurles Pierce Molony.

The Thurles Pierce says, 'My father had three brothers; all four boys were born in our family home here and all four became doctors. One of them, Uncle Jim, is alive and still attends the races. Both my parents rode as amateurs, but my grandfather was 6 ft 3 in., so he didn't ride, but he did have a permit to train.'

The current Pierce was also an amateur and he rode a winner, Summer Again, on his own track. It is an attractive course, with a fair hill sweeping away from the stable area and well-made fences, mostly with a short run between a pair of fences, followed by a long run to the next pair. In the distance is the Devil's Bit Mountain. Legend has it that the Devil, in a fit of temper, took a bite from the mountain and spat it out at Cashel, forming the famous rock.

The runners are silhouetted on the skyline (another pair of fences) and carry on right-handed towards the three-mile start, behind which, set among the trees, is the Molony family home. From here it is downhill over the last two fences or flights, and then a slight rise to the winning post.

It is a course that caters for the industry during the winter rather than for holidaymakers; its first meeting in September is all flat, and from there it is

two NH meetings per month from November through to March. Its pre-Christmas meeting stages the Horse and Jockey Hotel Listed Hurdle, sponsored by the nearby hostelry whose proprietor, Tom Egan, is a keen racing man. The traditional Church Holiday meeting in early January features the Heineken Phil Sweeney Memorial Listed Chase.

The second January meeting is one of Ireland's important pre-Cheltenham trials with both the Kinloch Brae Chase (Grade 2) and the Anaglogs Daughter Chase (Grade 3), both of which more in a moment. The most valuable race of all at Thurles is its first March meeting with the €62,000 Michael Purcell Memorial Hurdle (Grade 3).

On my visit in early December the fog only just cleared in time to allow the first race to start on schedule. It is a typical industry day and most of the spectators have some connection or another with the runners, of which there are plenty for the seven races: three steeplechases, three hurdles and a bumper.

The feature race is the three-mile Glen Steeplechase in which the Arthur Moore-trained Marcus Du Berlais, runner-up in the Irish Grand National, is a tentative tip. The field of six is a well bred lot. Two, The Galway Man and Baily Mist, are both by Zaffaran; the Paddy Mullins runner Cad A Ra Leat, owned and bred by Paddy's wife, Maureen, is by Shahrastani; Willie

J.P. McManus presents the trophy for the Martinstown Opportunity Handicap Steeplechase, with trainer T.J. O'Mara and jockey Tom Ryan

Mullins' runner Glacial Moss is by Glacial Storm; and Jessica Harrington's runner, Well Presented, is by another popular NH sire, Presenting. In the end it is Baily Mist, ridden by 3 lb claimer A.P. Lane, who wins from Well Presented and Marcus Du Berlais.

Champion-trainer Noel Meade wins the next, a two-mile hurdle, with a Key Of Luck gelding called Rolling Home ridden by Paul Carberry, completing a double for the jockey following his win in the beginners chase for Michael Hourigan on The Screamer.

The Rock of Cashel Hurdle is perhaps the most interesting for it includes

Hedgehunter runs in a hurdle race in December '04 in preparation for his successful launch at the 2005 Aintree Grand National

Hedgehunter, who was sharing the lead in the spring's Aintree Grand National when he fell at the last fence. Paul Carberry is the rider today for trainer Willie Mullins and watching him walk round the paddock, he looks all over a chaser. He runs well in this two-mile six-furlong hurdle, but is tapped for toe at the end when victory goes, surprisingly, to the 50–1 outsider Dalvento for owner/trainer John Joseph Murphy and 7 lb-claiming rider W.O. Callaghan.

One of the stewards here at Thurles is Lieutenant Colonel L. Kiely, who showjumped for Ireland in his time.

Thurles is not afraid to be innovative

and back in 1969 the late Willie O'Grady approached Paddy Molony, the current incumbent's father, with a particular problem. Local trainer Willie had a nice young rising star for Anne, Duchess of Westminster called Kinloch Brae, but he couldn't find a suitable conditions chase pre-Cheltenham. He was afraid he would have to run him in a hurdle, which he didn't want to do. Various heads were brought together: Pierce Molony was delegated to meet the late Max Fleming who was clerk of the course at the time; the late Paddy Sleator, known for being good at producing handicap winners, was asked to advise on suitable weights; local owner and businessman Joe Murphy was asked to sponsor the race; and finally the National Hunt Committee was asked to authorise it.

The result was a £1,000 conditions chase confined to horses trained locally in Munster; it was the biggest NH prize outside of the Dublin tracks at the time.

And the inaugural race was duly won by Kinloch Brae. He was subsequently installed favourite for the 1970 Cheltenham Gold Cup and was bowling along in the lead until he fell three out, the notorious slightly downhill fence that has caught out many a contender. It was still an Irish horse that won, L'Escargot gaining the first of his two wins for Dan Moore and jockey Tommy Carberry.

A horse that made the Kinloch Brae his own in the early years of the new

millennium was Native Upmanship. A relaxed, laid-back chestnut gelding by Be My Native out of a Deep Run mare, he has, at the time of writing, won 16 races for owner Mrs John Magnier and trainer Arthur Moore. In his early days, when he was unbeaten over fences and obviously possessed stamina as well as speed, he was considered a Cheltenham Gold Cup horse, but in reality he proved more of an easy two-and-a-half/three-mile horse and it was only in 2005 that the newly extended Cheltenham Festival finally provided a championship race to suit that type: the *Daily Telegraph* Chase over two and a half miles.

Native Upmanship won the 2002 Melling Chase at Aintree and other good races, but he became a Kinloch Brae specialist at Thurles. He won it in 2002, '03 and '04, all of them at odds-on, a hat-trick that was applauded by the local punters. In 2002, ridden by Barry Cash, he beat Wicked Crack by ten lengths, in '03 at odds of 1–4 and ridden by Conor O'Dwyer, he beat Arctic Copper, and his '04 scalp was David's Lad.

In the 2005 running, victory went to the gallant Rathgar Beau, a racing-club horse trained by Eamon 'Dusty' Sheehy and ridden by Shay Barry; a performance good enough to put him in line for a tilt at the new *Daily Telegraph* Chase. A big horse, with a big gallop and a big heart too, Rathgar Beau was pulling double into the last fence of the Kinloch Brae, quickly

putting the likes of Central House and Nil Desperandum, no slouches themselves, behind him. Native Upmanship finished a gallant fourth, but it was thought his best days were almost certainly now behind him. Sulking before being pulled up at Cheltenham, retirement was more than ever on the cards, but he ran again at Navan in April 2005. In the three-horse race, Rathgar Beau was 4–1 on to win, but Native Upmanship led from flag-fall and, clearly enjoying himself, just kept on pulling out more for a popular victory. He ran a cracker at Punchestown, too, and Arthur Moore said, 'He'll tell us when he wants to retire.'

The conditions of the Kinloch Brae chase proved to be so good that they

Dalvento was a 50–1 winner of the Rock of Cashel Hurdle, Thurles; W.O. Callaghan up

remained unchanged until the Turf Club became computerised.

* * *

On 17 October 1991 a big, raw four year old made his racecourse debut at Thurles in a welter flat race, a type of professionals' bumper. As he was the outsider of the two Dermot Weld runners, stable jockey Mick Kinane had elected to ride the more fancied one.

All Mick saw during the race was the big, chestnut backside of his mount's stable companion, ridden by Pat Shanahan, as the pair pulled further and

further ahead. He trotted up by eight lengths at 20–1. It was impressive, but, even so, no one on that day had any inkling of what the horse would go on to achieve. A Melbourne Cup and 14 other wins later, Vintage Crop had become one of Ireland's most popular and courageous of flat horses.

Vintage Crop could have been expected to be an NH horse (he did actually run in Granville Again's Champion Hurdle in 1993). After his initial run at Thurles, he went straight to hurdling, winning two out of two at Fairyhouse and Leopardstown in December 1991. But when he reappeared the following May, it was back to flat racing and, bar that one attempt at Cheltenham for the Champion Hurdle, sponsored by his owner, Michael Smurfit, it was on the Flat that he remained, winning or placing in 20 of his 25 starts.

Vintage Crop lives in regal retirement at the National Stud near Kildare, with Danoli as his devoted companion. If he could see it, he would approve of the life-size statue erected in his honour overlooking The Curragh paddock. And he is not forgotten by the people of Thurles, either.

A statue of Vintage Crop, one of Ireland's favourite horses, who began his career at Thurles

FEBRUARY

LEOPARDSTOWN

'And they're turning into the home straight, they're neck and neck now, these two great rivals, there's not an inch between them . . .'

Nip and tuck, neither one giving way, stride for stride, the two great horses remained locked in combat the whole way up the two-and-three-quarter-furlong straight. Ridden by two of the finest jockeys in the world, Frankie Dettori and Mick Kinane, both riding at their magnificent best, willing on their mounts, urging, using every sinew of their fit bodies in their efforts to exhort their mounts to use theirs. And how they did, both horses responding courageously, giving of their best, digging into their deepest reserves and then more. Fantastic Light and Galileo. All the way up that long straight neither, to the human eye, could be seen as leading the other.

On their previous clash, in the King George VI and Queen Elizabeth Stakes at Royal Ascot, Galileo had prevailed. Unbeaten, he was odds-on to keep that record now. It is Leopardstown and at the finish of the Champion Stakes 2001, a photograph is called. In terms of sheer bravery and ability, neither horse deserved to lose. Those associated with both horses hovered around the winner's enclosure.

It was a race that thousands of people drove many miles to see; to be part of the experience, to feel the atmosphere and to witness the race first-hand rather than rely on the TV. OK, the pictures are superb, but you can't hear the sounds, see the scenes, smell, breathe in the air. Eighteen thousand in all, more than for any other flat meeting in Ireland bar the Irish Derby.

Three of the seven runners were representatives of Tipperary trainer Aidan O'Brien and two of Saeed Bin Suroor. The respective pacemakers had done their job, and Suroor's Give The Slip had moved over to let stable mate Fantastic Light slip through on his inside. Galileo had to take the wider route. The Champion Stakes is run over one and a quarter miles, a step back in distance for Galileo, but it was a distance both protagonists had won over.

Then came the verdict. Fantastic Light by a head. I'm deliberately not saying that he gained his revenge, for this would not be a word in the two horses' vocabulary were they able to speak. It was a race that is still remembered and will be for many years to come.

Leopardstown's chief executive Matt O'Dwyer, a former amateur rider whose previous business had been in the hospitality industry, was in his first year at the course at the time. He remembers simply, 'It was a phenomenal race.'

Galileo, a Sadler's Wells colt, was trained by Aidan O'Brien, owned by Mrs John Magnier and Michael Tabor, and ridden by Mick Kinane. Able to run only once in the autumn of his two-year-old career due to a persistent cough, he was unbeaten coming into this race, with the

Urban Sea, dam of Galileo, at the Irish National Stud

big three tally of the Epsom and Irish Derbys and the King George, traditionally the first occasion Derby winners take on their seniors and in which he had beaten Fantastic Light.

Fantastic Light ran many more times and was a model of consistency, and also raced in many different countries: England, Ireland, Dubai, the USA, Japan and Hong Kong. He travelled to Japan again for what should have been his last race, but was unable to run; I remember seeing him a few days later, newly arrived at stud in Newmarket, where he looked a picture.

Trained first by Sir Michael Stoute and then by Saeed Bin Suroor for Godolphin, Fantastic Light was American-bred out of a Nijinsky mare; he won twelve races and placed in eight more from twenty-five starts;

he was twice second in the King George, but he won in Nad Al Sheba (Dubai), Belmont Park (USA), Sha Tin (Hong Kong) and, of course, in Ireland, not only in Leopardstown but also on The Curragh.

Leopardstown, for its sheer class of racing, is the jewel in Irish racing's crown, both flat and jumping. For titan finishes between top-class horses it has no superior, and in the Champion Stakes in September it has a World Series race that, year on year, fully lives up to its name.

The €1 million Champion Stakes became part of the World Series in 1999. The series now takes in thirteen races in ten countries – Hong Kong, Singapore, Britain, USA, Japan, Australia, Germany, France, Ireland and Canada. Three of its Leopardstown winners have gone on to be world champion: Daylami in 1999, Fantastic Light in 2001 and High Chaparral in 2003. The 2004 winner at Leopardstown, Azamour, was watched by his owner, the Aga Khan, from a helicopter above the course, his flight into Ireland having been delayed. The helicopter bringing him to Leopardstown was unable to land until after the race was over. In July '05 Azamour won the King George VI and Queen Elizabeth Stakes at Royal Ascot at York.

The 2003 running of the Champion Stakes was another rightly heralded as the race of the season, between two Derby winners: High Chaparral, the hero of 2002, and representing that year, Alamshar.

This race did not quite go according to script.

Alamshar, fresh from his convincing Ascot victory over Sulamani and his courageous beating of Dalakhani in the Irish Derby, was installed favourite. He was one of three three year olds in the contest, along with France, Aidan O'Brien's pacemaker for High Chaparral, and the filly Vintage Tipple, who was supplemented following her hugely popular Irish Oaks win for Paddy Mullins. The three four year olds were High Chaparral, Dubai World Cup-winner Moon Ballad and the filly Islington. There was one five year old in the race, Falbrav, an exceptionally strong, tough horse, sometimes described as like a bull, who from two to four years raced in the south of France. Coming to Luca Cumani as a five year old, he added to his tally in several different countries, ending his career with a total of eight Group 1 wins over a variety of distances, thirteen wins in all and ten places from twenty-six starts. Of only three unplaced runs, two were at Ascot, and in one of those, Alamshar was the winner.

Yet again the Irish Champion Stakes provided a thrilling spectacle with an epic finish, and this time it was the older horses that held sway, the verdict going to High Chaparral by a neck from Falbrav, though he had to survive both an objection and a stewards' inquiry, a disappointing end to an outstanding race.

Alamshar was two lengths behind the winner in fourth.

* * *

In 1968 the Racing Board (now Horse Racing Ireland) acquired Leopardstown and saved the site from what would otherwise have been almost inevitably housing development. And way back in 1971 it was one of the first Irish courses to initiate refurbishments. From then on, it has been one of Europe's foremost racetracks.

But from its inception it was never considered a laggard, for the building of it in 1888 was modelled along the lines of Sandown Park on the fringes of London. With the demise of Baldoyle in the 1960s and Phoenix Park in the 1980s, Leopardstown is now the only Dublin-based track, being six miles south of the city centre, and is served by a motorway that runs right past it. There are also the Luas, the city's new tram system, built on the former Harcourt Street railway line that, until the 1960s, used to stop at Leopardstown; the Dart, the rail system; and a special race-day bus service as alternative transport.

Although racing is Leopardstown's *raison d'être*, it has become a thriving leisure facility, pandering to many types of people and activity, from its 18-hole golf course (which has 2,000 female members) and 48-bay floodlit driving range inside

the race circuit, to its large health and fitness centre and popular nightclub, Club 92, open four nights a week. On race days, Club 92 becomes one of the four bars, while among the eating facilities the Fillies Café Bar is, like the nightclub, open all year round, as is the newly launched Fado's Celtic cuisine restaurant.

The Curragh hosts all five Irish Classics, but Leopardstown holds, as we have seen, the World Series Champion Stakes in September. It also stages the Derby Trial in May. This is another race that lives up to its billing, for its winners from 2000 have been Sinndar, Galileo, High Chaparral, Alamshar and, in 2004, Yeats. The first three went on to win the Epsom Derby, while Alamshar clinched the Irish Derby. But what makes Leopardstown so special is that it also hosts many of the country's leading NH races and, because the track holds 22 meetings per annum, visitors can enjoy racing here, in the Dublin suburbs and close to the foothills of the Wicklow Mountains, at any time of year.

For many, it is December, January and February that cannot be missed. The Christmas Festival includes the Lexus (formerly Ericsson) Chase; January sees the AIG Europe Champion Hurdle, as well as the prestigious Pierse Hurdle; and February brings not only pre-Cheltenham trials, but also one of Ireland's jumping Classics, the Hennessy Cognac Gold Cup.

Jodami, the Cheltenham Gold Cup winner of 1993, won the race three times:

in 1993 when he beat Chatham by a head, again in 1994, beating Deep Bramble, and then in 1995, when he beat Merry Gale. By Crash Course, Jodami was trained in Yorkshire by Peter Beaumont who liked bringing him over to Ireland, being placed in Punchestown and Fairyhouse also. He returned once more to Leopardstown in February 1997 for his swansong, when he was second in his favourite race to Danoli.

Even Jodami's great record was eclipsed by Florida Pearl, who won the race a magnificent four times. Owned by Mrs Violet O'Leary and trained throughout his career by Willie Mullins, the big, white-faced Florida Pearl made Leopardstown his stamping ground. In a thirty-three-race career he won sixteen times, and of those runs twelve were at Leopardstown, where he scored eight times. Three of his first four runs were on the Dublin track, a win in the Cheltenham Festival bumper being sandwiched in-between. He went straight from bumpers to novice chasing; he won his first in December beating Delphi Lodge and his second when he beat Boss Doyle at Leopardstown prior to taking the Royal & SunAlliance Novices Chase at Cheltenham. The Gold Cup eluded him, though he was second and third in it. Back at Leopardstown in February 1999 he scored the first of his memorable Hennessys, beating L'Escartefigue by two lengths. Placings at Cheltenham, Punchestown and Leopardstown followed, then in January 2000, at Leopardstown

The presence of triple Gold Cup-winner Best Mate was a big draw at Leopardstown's Christmas meeting. Visiting fans show where their allegiance lies

again, he beat Amberleigh House, the 2004 Grand National winner, by a short head. A month later he was back for his second Hennessy in which he beat Dorans Pride, and the following year he made it three in a row, joining Jodami in the hat-trick. That he came back three years later with, by his standards, a lean spell in-between (interrupted by niggling injuries and ailments) to win a fourth Hennessy Cognac Gold Cup in February 2004, ranks up there not only with the great training feats but also as an example of sheer courage in adversity from a horse. Although it had been hoped to have one more crack at the Gold Cup, this

Mrs Jim Lewis, wife of Best Mate's owner

Leopardstown race became, in the end, his highly fitting finale.

In 1998 Dorans Pride was successful for Michael Hourigan, who trained Beef Or Salmon to win the Ericsson (now Lexus) in 2002 (as a five year old) and 2004. In the intervening year it went to Best Mate, English-owned and trained by Jim Lewis and Henrietta Knight, but Irish-bred in Co. Meath by Jaques Van't Hart.

When Best Mate first took part in 2003, surprisingly bypassing the King George at Kempton Park on Boxing Day, Beef Or Salmon was the holder, but Best Mate had won the last two runnings of the Cheltenham Gold Cup. Running and jumping superbly, Best Mate won effortlessly, his stepping stone to his third Gold Cup. Beef Or Salmon, who gurgled

during the race, was only third, but in 2004 it was a different story for the renewal. The preliminaries were similar: there was again a wintry sun dappling the paddock, the crowd was again in the order of 20,000 and owner Jim Lewis could once more be seen walking round the pre-parade ring with his horse while chatting to Best Mate's lass. Henrietta Knight again disappeared away from the crowds while the race was in progress.

At the very first fence, Best Mate nearly sprawled on landing. There was no gasp from the crowd and no mention of it from the commentator, so I began to think I'd imagined it until a few days later when jockey Jim Culloty told *At The Races* that

Henrietta Knight retreats to her hiding place

Best Mate 'had done the splits' at the first. But the pace was steady and by the end of the first circuit the champion had strolled into the lead, stalked by Beef Or Salmon, who joined him at the last fence first time round. With two fences to go the writing was on the wall for Best Mate. Paul Carberry pressed the button on Beef Or Salmon and received an immediate response; Jim Culloty found Best Mate's tank uncharacteristically empty and as Beef Or Salmon soared over the last fence in a clear lead it was Rule Supreme who looked the challenger for second place, only to crumple on landing. So Best Mate retained his never-out-of-the-first-two record while Paul Carberry turned in the saddle and beckoned 'come on' to his great rival, a humorous gesture between two friends but viewed dimly by the stewards. Two days after the race Best Mate was found to be coughing and, eventually, he had to forego his attempt at a fourth Gold Cup in which it was the turn of Beef Or Salmon to be found to be ailing.

A month after the Ericsson, Leopards-town staged the Hennessy Cognac Gold Cup where Beef Or Salmon and Rule Supreme renewed rivalry, and again there was a surprise in store, for this time Rule Supreme ran on the stronger. This gave trainer Willie Mullins success for the sixth time in the last seven runnings of this

Life's a laugh: seen here sharing a joke are Tom Gallagher and the love of his equine life, Vinnie Roe, who won on his debut as a two year old at Leopardstown

contest. It was also great for jockey David Casey, who had only recently returned to race-riding after breaking a leg.

It seems that whatever the day at Leopardstown, be it flat or jumping, it can always be relied on to serve up triumphant stories and exciting racing that gets the crowds buzzing and wanting to come back for more.

NAAS

At only 20 miles from Dublin and set in the heart of the thoroughbred county of Kildare, Naas has so much going for it: a proud history, top names among its winners, big improvements to facilities in the last decade with ambitious plans for more, and lots of fun summer barbecue evenings as well as its more serious fixtures.

Yet there may be a question mark hanging over its future.

The agreed route for a new road, around which Naas racecourse built its smart new developments, has now been changed by the powers that be to a line that would cross part of the car park, causing a considerable problem that has to be resolved. It is very bad luck for a management that is forward thinking and efficient – especially coming, as it does, after much of their refurbishment has already been completed, most recently the widening of the track to 100 metres ready for 2006.

It was in 1922 that local businessmen and farmers Thomas Whelan, Charles Farrell, Edward Brophy, Edward Dowling, Patrick Berney and a few others got together to create a course at Naas. They were rewarded with an excellent inaugural mixed meeting on 19 June 1924 and it was a tribute to their ambition that 80 years later, on 16 June 2004, Naas hosted its first-ever Group race.

This was the Irish Stallion Farms European Breeders Fund Noblesse Stakes

While the bookmakers set up for the day, potential punters relax

(Group 3) worth €90,000 and was won by Danelissima, bred and trained by Jim Bolger in Coolcullen, Co. Carlow, and owned by his wife. The delighted trainer said afterwards that he would aim the Danehill filly for the Irish Oaks. Danelissima deserved to appear in the top races, but in the end the Naas race was her only win in ten runs.

Two years earlier the course had staged the richest two-year-old Listed fillies race in Europe, the Swordlestown Stud Sprint Trophy over six furlongs, worth €80,000. This was enough to tempt Richard Hannon over from Salisbury Plain in Wiltshire, England, to score with Ragtop, ridden by Dane O'Neill for owner Fergus Jones. Bred in Ireland by K. Molloy, Ragtop was completing a hat-trick from as many runs when she won at Naas and came back to Ireland, to The Curragh, for win number four later in the year.

Frank Ennis landed the Swordlestown Stud Sprint with Miss Childrey, ridden by Seamus Heffernan, in 2003, and the impressive 2004 winner was the exciting filly Damson, owned by Mrs John Magnier and Michael Tabor. Ridden by Jamie Spencer, Damson beat Pictavia by a convincing two lengths.

Damson ran five times that year, winning four. Initially she won over five furlongs at Cork and then the Naas race over six, after which trainer David Wachman said that although she was a smart filly, he did not put Royal Ascot on the agenda. 'I have given her time and will look for a Group race. She has done the job well today.'

She continued to do the job so well that David Wachman changed his mind, sent her to Royal Ascot for the 17-runner Queen Mary Stakes (Group 2) over five furlongs and won it, beating Soar by three lengths, prompting her trainer to say, 'I didn't know what a Queen Mary winner looked like, but I do now!'

The bay by Entrepreneur, out of a mare who won over one and a quarter miles in France, cost €160,000. She continued to repay the investment when landing a valuable Group 1 race over six furlongs on The Curragh that August, where both her speed and stamina were evident. Her only defeat came at Newmarket in September, when she was third, beaten half a length.

* * *

Naas has seen many marvellous National Hunt horses over the years and was the scene of Mill House's first win, when he took the Osberstown Hurdle in 1961. A year later, Arkle won the Rathconnell Hurdle at Naas. It was his first handicap and it was also the first time he was ridden in a race by Pat Taaffe. In a field of ten, he carried third-top weight and, though 'green' (i.e. a novice), justified 2–1 favouritism to score by four lengths.

Naas, set in the heart of the 'thoroughbred county', Co. Kildare, only 20 miles from Dublin

Maytime Adventure leads the way from Rinceshane (number 5) at an early flight in a maiden hurdle

Another to win here was Silver Fame, who went on to win ten races at Cheltenham, a record that still stands, for Lord Bicester in the early 1950s.

The one-and-a-half-mile oval track at Naas has two long sides, making it suitable for a long-striding, galloping horse, and a steady uphill home straight. For the flat racers, it has both a five- and six-furlong straight.

Naas has been graced by future Aintree Grand National winners as well as hosting Cheltenham Festival hopefuls. Kilmore, Team Spirit, Nicolaus Silver and Early Mist all scored at Naas before going on to Aintree glory, and more recently this has been the route of Monty's Pass. He ran in a hurdle race here as his prep race for his 2003 win and his 2004 fourth in the Aintree Grand National.

It attracts the top jockeys under either code, including the Carberry family.

* * *

Paul Carberry is 'the best jockey in the world, but not always the easiest to keep in check', so says Noel Meade, for whom Paul has ridden for most of his career – bar two brief spells during his flat-race apprenticeship.

Irrepressible, Paul has a wicked sense of fun and humour, and a devil-may-care attitude. Less than two weeks before the 2005 Cheltenham Festival he attempted to jump an iron gate whilst out hunting, but

failed, the horse fell and rolled on top of him.

It is well known that Paul's love of hunting is something he is not willing to compromise, and he lets it be known that he doesn't take race-rides on Tuesdays or Fridays, the days in winter when he whips in to the Ward Union Staghounds.

There was a day when racing at Wexford was postponed from a Sunday to the following Friday. This can happen sometimes for reasons such as waterlogging. Paul's agent told Noel Meade that Paul could not ride, as the new date was a Friday, sacrosanct in Paul's diary. He is a law unto himself, and his exceptional ability keeps his services in demand. However, on this occasion, Noel said that unless the horse was balloted out, Paul, as his retained jockey, had to ride. Just to make sure, Noel drove Paul down in his car himself.

The horse was called Open Range and in the paddock the owners Paul and Lynn Shanahan asked Noel if he thought it would win.

'I hope so,' Noel replied.

'Not half as much as I do,' Paul muttered under his breath, thinking of the day's hunting he was missing.

Luckily Open Range won.

Paul will always try his hardest. There was a time when he beat a young Best Mate in a Cheltenham hurdle race on Sausalito Bay. Jim Culloty took a lot of stick for being beaten that day, but Noel

Meade says that Paul had been unable to 'ride' Sausalito Bay from the top of the hill.

'At the top of the hill Paul felt an excruciating pain across his back; he thought he'd been struck by a whip, but, in fact, it was a haematoma, caused by a kick in a fall, that burst. He was unable to ride again for the rest of the festival.'

Noel goes on, 'He's a genius; for all his madness, he is an absolute genius. When he's on song, there's no one better anywhere. He rides from a gift, he's something special.

'His father, Tommy, was a riding genius, too, and his mother, Pamela, is daughter of Dan Moore, sister to Arthur, so it was bred into Paul.'

Tommy Carberry won five Irish

Paul Carberry, a riding genius

37

riding championships and was twice Champion Apprentice; he won three Gold Cups (on L'Escargot and Ten Up), the Grand National on L'Escargot, and two Irish Nationals (on Brown Lad).

Paul himself has so far won the Irish National (in 1998) and a year later the Grand National, both on Bobbyjo, trained by his father. And although Paul won two races at the 2005 Cheltenham Festival, there was no better sight than at the end of the Fred Winter Handicap Hurdle when the unplaced Paul kissed the winning rider – his highly talented sister, Nina!

Neat, with a great sense of timing, judge of pace and an eye for a fence that has been with her since her Pony Club days, Nina has been welcomed into the riders' ranks. And then there is Philip. He, too, has inherited the family race-riding ability and in a hurdle race on Irish Grand National day 2005, with Paul fallen on the ground somewhere out in the country and victory looking likely for Nina on the top-weighted favourite, it was Philip whose turn it was for a pillar-to-post victory.

* * *

On 31 October 1992 a little bay gelding by The Parson made his racing debut in a bumper at Naas. Seventeen went to post and the Thomas Foley-trained debutant started at odds of 16–1. Ridden by

amateur Mr P. English, he scored by a length.

Exactly three months later he reappeared at Naas for his second run and was still a 10–1 outsider in a field of 15. This time, his winning margin was four lengths.

Danoli had come on the scene. He captured the hearts of the racing public and is naturally special to Naas.

Named after his joint owners Dan and Olive O'Neill, he was trained throughout his illustrious career by Tom Foley in Co. Carlow. After those two initial Naas successes, Danoli made it a five-timer, at Punchestown twice and Fairyhouse, three bumpers and two hurdles. After a third and second place, both at Leopardstown, he then notched up another five-timer, including at the Cheltenham Festival and at Aintree, in Grade 1 hurdles. A year later he was third in Alderbrook's Champion Hurdle and repeated his success at Aintree. For his countless fans, his best remembered race is the 1997 Hennessy Cognac Gold Cup in which, as a novice, he denied English raider Jodami his fourth win in the race. The commentator's voice was drowned by the noise of the crowds, and it remains a race that stands out in many people's memories.

In his 32-race career, he was only once unplaced when standing up (when he was fourth in Collier Bay's Champion Hurdle) and fell or unseated five times.

Danoli had another win at Naas, in a novice chase, and in his fourth and final

appearance at the Co. Kildare track he was second in a Grade 2 chase. He was a great favourite with the Irish crowds and now enjoys a blissful retirement with Vintage Crop at the Irish National Stud near Kildare.

Naas – *Nas na Riogh* – 'the meeting place of Kings'. Let's hope Naas racecourse will be able to continue to host the Sport of Kings.

A smiling Nina Carberry at Laytown, September 2005, where she rode a winner

MARCH

CHELTENHAM

Cheltenham. The very word breathes magic in the air. Sends a tingle down the spine. This is the meeting that all in NH racing on both sides of the Irish Sea have built up to and lived for over the last 12 months since the previous festival.

And of all the festivals, this is *the* festival. The test. The best. More than anywhere else in the world, it is every owner's ambition to have a winner at the Cheltenham National Hunt Festival. And to win the Queen Mother Champion Chase, the Smurfit Champion Hurdle or, crème de la crème, the totesport Cheltenham Gold Cup is the highest accolade of all.

The build-up in Ireland is intense for weeks beforehand, and not just in the racing columns either. Horse-racing news is on both the national television and radio bulletins several times a week. From mid-February onwards there are various special Cheltenham preview evenings, ranging in venue from the local pub to smart hotels in all quarters of the island and the Mansion House, the Lord Mayor's residence, in the centre of Georgian Dublin. Usually the sponsor is a bookmaker and the beneficiary a charity – and, of course, the *raison d'être* of the evening: there is always a panel of experts, including some from England, to give their tips for Cheltenham. Names like Edward O'Grady, Jessica Harrington, Paul Carberry, Noel Meade, Tony Mullins,

Sumptuous hampers come out pre-
Cheltenham

As the crowds arrive for the festival, a light
plane advertises totesport's sponsorship of
the Cheltenham Gold Cup

Dessie Hughes, Tom Taaffe, Barry Geraghty and Tom Foley are among those from the 'home' side at various venues. From across the water come Philip Hobbs, Nigel Twiston-Davies, Alan King, Mick Fitzgerald, Johnny Francome, Jim Culloty and Tony McCoy to add their opinions. Chairmen include racing journalists like Tony O'Hehir, Richard Pitman, Leo Powell and Ted Walsh. The evenings are not only entertaining, but also informative, with useful tips for the forthcoming festival for the hundreds of punters who fill the halls at these occasions.

Most of Ireland remains riveted for the four days (three until 2004). Some 10,000 Irishmen cram into the classy spa town of Cheltenham, the B&Bs in surrounding villages, the hotels and the pubs; especially the pubs. Several thousand more who already live in England attend too. Those left behind in Ireland hold Cheltenham parties, sitting glued to the telly in their local pub or at a house party in a friend's home.

This is their fun, their holiday, their craic. And they intend to make a few bob out of it too. Managing director Edward Gillespie and 5,500 staff intend to make it run smoothly for all-comers. Tote turnover for this meeting is higher even than for Royal Ascot, due in part, no doubt, to the Irish influence. Some 125,000 pints of Guinness will be drunk, along with 8,000 bottles of champagne, 20,000 bottles of wine, 150,000 pints of draught beer or lager, and another 24,000 bottles of beer. Blotting paper comes in the form of 14,000 portions of chips, 20,000 beef burgers and hot dogs, and 47,000 sandwiches. Music from an Irish band

plays throughout the meeting in the Guinness village.

Nearly every other voice in the crowd is Irish, it seems, including a number of priests and, as this meeting nearly always coincides with St Patrick's Day, there are a number of shamrock sellers too. In Ireland, Paddy's Day is a Bank Holiday, so thousands of people are legitimately watching Cheltenham instead of working.

It is the end of the first day and security guards are ushering out the few remaining people in the Guinness tented village, shutting up shop behind them, chivvying stragglers as they go. It is beginning to look like a ghost town. That is until they come to the Brave Inca suite. Far from going home, this tent is still overflowing, its happy, inebriated, celebratory owners, the seven-man Novices Syndicate, and their numerous friends spilling out into the corridor. They have been here since the first race of the first day of the 2004 festival. Their horse has done it. By a whisker. The Supreme Novices Hurdle. Brave Inca. His owners and supporters came here to back him. And to toast him. And to celebrate. No member of security staff is about to turf them out.

There is friendly rivalry and considerable banter between the British and the Irish concerning the merits of their respective horses. Whose is the best? Over the next few days this pinnacle of NH racing worldwide will give the answers.

Even the English-trained winners are likely to be ridden by an Irish jockey: Tony McCoy, Tony Dobbin, Mick Fitzgerald, Graham Lee, Ruby Walsh, Barry Fenton, Jim Culloty et al. And it is the retired Richard Dunwoody, an Ulsterman like Tony McCoy, who has ridden more winners than any other jockey at Cheltenham, a total of 109.

Before 2005 the last Irish-trained winner of the totesport Gold Cup was Imperial Call in 1996, though nearly every other winner since then has been Irish-bred, notably Best Mate.

The Irish have twice had seven winners at the festival, slightly over one third of the total, in 1977 and again 20 years later. There have been so many good Irish winners at Cheltenham over the decades that there is not room to mention them all. But Arkle won the Broadway Novices Chase in 1963, and then the following three Cheltenham Gold Cups; Best Mate has won three Gold Cups; and the outstanding mare was Dawn Run, who won the Champion Hurdle in 1984 and, in one of the greatest races, the Gold Cup two years later. She is still the only horse to have won both, though others have tried.

In earlier times, in the 1930s, Golden Miller won five Gold Cups. Arkle's trainer, Tom Dreaper, won the 1946 Gold Cup with Prince Regent, and two years after Arkle he won it again with Fort Leney. In-between it was the young genius Vincent O'Brien, from the green fields of

Tipperary, who sent out Cottage Rake for his three memorable Gold Cups (1948–50), as well as Hatton's Grace for his three Champion Hurdles (1949–51), and another Gold Cup with Knock Hard, before turning his mastery to the Flat.

In the 1970s Dan Moore trained L'Escargot to win two Gold Cups. Glencaraig Lady was a rare winner on the distaff side, trained by Francis Flood. And Tom Dreaper's son, Jim, was in charge of Ten Up. This was a great decade for Irish-trained Gold Cup winners, with Mick O'Toole's charge, Davy Lad, scoring in 1977, while the Champion Hurdle winner of 1978 and '79 was the little battler Monksfield, trained by Des McDonogh.

Dan Moore trained Quita Que to win

Visitors enjoy the action from the Members' Lawn and grandstand

the first Queen Mother Champion Chase, over two miles, in 1959, and then it was Tom Dreaper's Fortria twice, followed by Ben Stack, Flyingbolt, Muir and Straight Fort over the next decade from the Meath maestro. Sons Jim Dreaper (Lough Inagh) and Arthur Moore (Drumgora) continued the good work while Fran Woods, son of Paddy Woods, who used to ride work on Arkle for Tom Dreaper, rode Klairon Davis to Queen Mother victory in 1996.

These days, tickets for the festival sell out two months in advance.

Because Cheltenham racecourse is set in such a mighty bowl and runners sweep away from spectators in the stands, it gives the impression of being an open, galloping course, but this is a misconception. Walk the course and it is quite tight, with sharp turns.

It is 2005. And what an incredible Cheltenham for the Irish. The big three: the Smurfit Champion Hurdle, Queen Mother Champion Chase and the totesport Cheltenham Gold Cup. For the first time ever they come back to Ireland in the same year.

Never before has there been an Irish hand like it for the Champion Hurdle. No less than seven Irish horses fill the top prices in the betting, Brave Inca among them. Can Hardy Eustace do it again for Dessie Hughes and Conor O'Dwyer? Or will it be the newly vaunted Macs Joy for Jessica Harrington with Barry Geraghty on

board? And then there is Harchibald, out of the top drawer, trained by Noel Meade and ridden by Paul Carberry. In the end Hardy Eustace and Edward O'Grady's charge, Back in Front (Ruby Walsh), go off joint favourites. The nearest English horse in the betting is Rooster Booster, and he is way out at 16–1. For all that he was runner-up last year and winner the year before.

It is Hardy Eustace, a proven stayer, who does it the hard way once more, leading from flag-fall, stretching his rivals' stamina to their limits. Over the last and on the run to the line, both Harchibald and Brave Inca look poised to go by, but the reigning champion holds on, to rapturous welcomes. The first five home are Irish.

Moscow Flyer regains the Two Mile crown he lost the previous year after dumping jockey Barry Geraghty and makes it 18 chase wins from 18 completions – more Irish flags and singsongs – and then Kicking King in the biggest one of all, and a double for Barry Geraghty, bringing scenes reminiscent of Arkle for trainer Tom Taaffe and legions of Irish hero-worshippers.

Then there's Spot Thedifference in the Sporting Index Cross Country race for trainer Enda Bolger; a jubilant Nina Carberry on 20–1 outsider Dabiroun for Paul Nolan in the Fred Winter (he would have been pleased) Juvenile Handicap Hurdle – what a tidy rider Nina is; Missed

The view from the top of the hill

That (Willie Mullins/Ruby Walsh) in the Weatherbys Champion Bumper; Oulart (Dessie Hughes/Paul Carberry) in the Pertemps Handicap Hurdle final; and finally Fota Island for Mouse Morris, Paul Carberry and owner J.P. McManus in the Johnny Henderson Grand Annual Handicap Chase. A record nine wins for the Irish – and some very special celebrations.

* * *

The Smurfit Champion Hurdle is sponsored by an Irish company, headed by Sir Michael Smurfit, who, as holder of both British and Irish citizenship, was knighted in the 2005 Queen's Birthday Honours list. He built up his business from 200 staff to 72,000, and from two factories to 700, in the ever-evolving packaging business. In earlier years it was his late brother Jeff who used to go to Cheltenham, while Michael stayed in Ireland working.

'Then I went one year and I just fell in love with it,' he recalls. 'Then Waterford Crystal [the previous sponsors of the Champion Hurdle] got in a bit of bother. I had got to know Edward Gillespie [Cheltenham MD] and Lord Vestey [Cheltenham chairman] and I knew they were keen to have an Irish sponsor.

'When it became available, I grabbed it. It is without doubt the best sponsorship to have; it's value for money and a wonderful three to four days. When there's an Irish winner, the place comes alive; the ethos and character is incomparable.

'When we sponsor golf and invite people, only some will come, but everyone who's asked comes to Cheltenham. The place grabs you, and we're in it for a long-term commitment.'

Michael's father, the late John Jefferson Smurfit, kept a few horses with the late Harry Keogh and Vincent O'Brien, whose second-ever winner belonged to Smurfit. Michael's father would take him racing as a lad, locally to Naas and to the Irish Grand National at Fairyhouse, but it was golf that he became keen on.

It was not until he discovered that his own son, Tony, was sneaking up to the bookmakers with his grandfather, and had been doing so for a number of years, that Michael took an interest in racing again.

He built a stud at Forenaghts near Naas, where Wolfe Tone was born, and had about 25 mares on its 300 acres. Of his horses in training most are with Dermot Weld, plus one or two with Arthur Moore, Jim Bolger and Willie Mullins, and the occasional one in France or America.

'I wouldn't count my breeding a success; we've yet to have a seriously good one,' he says, 'but it is a hobby, so is the racing, though the stud does pay for itself.'

His eldest son, Tony, is now chief operations officer of the Smurfit Group and chairman of Goffs, the international bloodstock sales company based in Co. Kildare, and he is also hands on at the stud, which he now owns.

Michael enjoys being involved in all aspects of racing and has put a considerable amount back into the sport that he loves. 'I used to be champion jumping owner before J.P. sent me into oblivion, but I have never been in the top ten on the Flat. I saw the potential for traditional flat horses to go into jumping and I got Dermot Weld involved.'

Michael's first big moment in racing came in the 1983 Grand National when his Greasepaint was second to Corbiere. 'He was second again, carrying 11 stone, the following year, to Hallo Dandy, and I turned to my son and said, "We might as well be on Mars or another planet, no one cares about second."'

He has won the Irish Grand National with Perris Valley in 1988 and the Triumph Hurdle at Cheltenham with Rare Holiday, both trained by Dermot Weld and ridden by Brendan Sheridan, who is now with the Turf Club. Michael also won the Galway Plate in 1990 with Kiichi, as well as General Idea in 1993. He once had the ante-post favourite for the Champion Hurdle, Fortune and Fame, which he co-owned with John Magnier, but he was cast in his box the night before and could not run. He ran four more times, notably beating Danoli in '94 in the Irish Champion Hurdle and gaining fourth in the '95 Champion Hurdle at Cheltenham, the year he won the Irish Champion Hurdle again.

But it is for some of his flat horses that Michael Smurfit is best known: Vintage Crop and Media Puzzle, both winners of the Melbourne Cup in Australia. He will also be remembered for not buying Grey Swallow, winner of the Irish Derby, because he was spun (failed the veterinary inspection, that is) for his wind at the sales.

Media Puzzle had to qualify for the Melbourne Cup, so, after his journey Down Under and spell in quarantine, he ran in the Geelong Cup and promptly won, breaking the course record.

But it is Vintage Crop that holds a special place in his heart. Michael cannot get to see all his horses run, sometimes even in the big races, because of pressure at work. He missed Vintage Crop's Melbourne Cup win in 1993 but was there for his third attempt (he was seventh in 1994) which he believes was one of the horse's greatest races.

'It was his best race and he was top weight. He missed the break but stormed through the field to finish third, it was a real cracker. He was a once-in-a-lifetime horse to own; he's my favourite and he gave me most pleasure. He made history with the incomparable Dermot Weld training him and the dynamic Mick Kinane riding him. I also saw him win his two St Legers.

'He is still alive and living at the National Stud where he receives thousands of visitors a year.' There is also a life-size statue of him at The Curragh beside the paddock. Michael unashamedly plays video recordings of his horses winning many times over.

Michael Smurfit was chairman of the Irish Racing Board for five years in the 1980s, during which time Sunday racing was introduced, as were computers. The model of Leopardstown, the Apprentice Centre and the Racing Board HQ were also designed.

'Racing in Ireland has become extremely popular, with private money injected and improved drainage, and the government has been far-sighted in granting decent money because it's a self-fulfilling thing, meaning less unemployment, more VAT, and it's self-funding.

'I enjoy my racing and I think the future's very bright for Irish racing: Irish horses are great, the sales are good, and J.P. can give half a million euros for a jumping horse. I can remember a time when decent Irish horses were sold to England, so Irish racing was in decline. I wouldn't go to see ordinary store horses run, but I always want to see the champions.'

But then, Michael Smurfit is a champion man.

* * *

The three best moments in racing for Curragh-based Dessie Hughes all came at Cheltenham: winning the Champion Hurdle as a rider on board Monksfield in 1979 and, 25 and 26 years later, in the Champion Hurdle again, this time as trainer of the 2004–05 winner, Hardy Eustace. But in-between he went through training hell and back.

There's an expression, 'To get caught by the racing bug'. Many will know the feeling. Riding, owning, betting – it's an addiction.

But for Dessie Hughes in the 1990s the saying took on a new meaning: for ten long years his yard was bitten by a bug of a different nature. Sick horses. Poor form. Disappearing owners. Twice all the horses were moved out. Got better. Improved form. Even won a bit. Returned. Ill again. Boxes had to be fumigated, tar had been burnt. Still the mystery bug survived. For

a decade. By then, just 15 of 80 horses remained.

'It nearly finished us,' Dessie recalls quietly.

One glimmer kept up his spirits and those of his wife, Eileen: their son, Richard, who was making a name for himself as a top-class jockey in England. The light comes back into Dessie's eyes. Richard had been champion pony racer at the age of 12. He left school at 15 to be apprenticed to his father, did well, then England called. He joined Richard Hannon on the edge of Salisbury Plain, and eventually married one of his daughters, too. 'He's been a great lift to us, a real buzz that got us through a difficult spell,' says Dessie.

'I think he'll stay in England.' His voice is a little wistful, tinged with pride. 'That's where all his contacts are now, and I expect he'll become a trainer in time.'

In 2005, Richard Hughes was there at Cheltenham with his father, walking in with hero Hardy Eustace.

Ten long years in the doldrums would have sunk many a trainer. The couple sold some of their land – 'We were lucky that we had an owner wanting some at the time' – so they did not have to sell the yard. One gets the feeling Dessie sees good in even the worst of times, and it helps.

Eventually Tom Buckley from the equine centre said there was a machine in his practice that was meant to detect strange viruses, but it had found nothing

in four years. So it was brought to Osborne Lodge, Dessie's yard on The Curragh, to try out. Swabs were taken from the walls and the machine nearly exploded with positives.

The problem was diagnosed as aspergillosis, normally associated with chickens and other birds. The boxes were all sprayed and fresh swabs were taken every month for a year until finally, at last, they came up negative.

Dessie Hughes was back.

Since then, the number of occupied boxes has risen to 50, and with them a loyal band of owners, not least Carlow businessman Lar Byrne. It was he who paid the comparatively modest figure of 22,000 guineas for a four year old by the sprinter Archway at the Goffs Land-Rover sale in June, Dessie having viewed him at the Limerick base of his breeders, Louise Cooper and Patrick Joyce, the previous November.

The advantage of waiting for the sale was that it made him eligible for the prestigious bumper in Punchestown the following spring. The gelding, by now named Hardy Eustace, duly won it in the hands of Dessie's amateur rider Roger Loughran, having first run in a maiden hurdle under Dessie's capable conditional jockey Kieran Kelly. He was a noteworthy sixth in the Champion Bumper at the Punchestown Festival and then turned out for his summer at grass at P.J. and Catherine Murphy's land in Walterstown,

Co. Westmeath. Catherine is Lar Byrne's sister.

The bay with black points and no white on him took it all in his stride. 'He's the kindest horse in the place; he eats, sleeps, and says "What do you want me to do?" and then tries to do it. He's the same every day. He eats the same amount of food and drinks the same amount of water, even if he's travelled and is staying away,' says Dessie. At home he is looked after and ridden out six days a week by his lad, amateur rider Robert Hennessy.

Dessie continues. 'The horse keeps his condition. I never have a day's worry with him, he's so laid-back. Even when Kieran Kelly won the Royal & SunAlliance Novices Hurdle with him at Cheltenham, he was kicking away at him before four

Dessie Hughes and Hardy Eustace

49

out; he only looked like winning after the last.' The only time that matters, of course.

That win was a great credit to Kieran Kelly, his first big milestone in what looked like a burgeoning career. Barely four months later he was cruelly killed in a racing fall at his home track of Kilbeggan. The small, tight-knit world of Irish racing was truly stunned and mourned his loss grievously. For some of his weighing-room colleagues it was particularly difficult, as well as for the owner and trainer of the horse, and for friends and lifelong acquaintances. But most of all for his family from the little village of Derrinturn, Co. Kildare.

Kieran had come to Dessie having already ridden one winner on the Flat, named, prophetically, Angel from Heaven. 'He was a good lad with talent, who always worked hard in the yard and was a very popular fellow.' It is a sentiment frequently echoed around the country.

After the Cheltenham win Dessie began to think he might have a future staying hurdler in Hardy Eustace. 'I didn't dream of the Champion Hurdle then, though the owner, Lar, had ideas,' laughs Dessie. 'I didn't think he'd have the speed for it.' But winning a one-mile six-furlong flat race in Navan the following October showed he had plenty of foot.

The route to the Champion Hurdle was not all plain sailing, and he might well have run in the Coral Cup instead. But, through a line with Solerina, George's Girl and Rhinestone Cowboy, the form for the Champion Hurdle was there for all with eyes to see it, for all his 33–1 starting price.

The reigning champion, the grey Rooster Booster with a fairy tale of his own to tell, was favourite. Hardy Eustace, at home over two and a half miles, set out to make the running to ensure a stamina test, but when he was joined by the favourite at the last, the grey looked certain to win. Not a bit of it. Hardy Eustace and Conor O'Dwyer dug deep together, determined not to let the grey by, and then, what's more, pulled out some more again to put five lengths between them at the line.

Lar Byrne, who runs a packaging depot and distribution centre in Tullow, Co. Carlow, had been quietly placing bets on his horse via the Internet at some incredibly long odds. His total outlay of €240 reaped him €62,000.

The euphoria that followed was tinged only with the sadness of knowing it should have been Kieran Kelly's ride and tributes were paid to him by owner, trainer and jockey alike.

Only regular lad, Robert Hennessy, was missing. He elected to ride in a point-to-point in Ireland instead, and fell. (But he was there at Cheltenham in 2005.)

Then came the rematch: Ireland's Champion Hurdle, held on the last day of the Punchestown Festival 2004. Had Cheltenham been a fluke? Dessie Hughes was confident about his charge and brought him there in tip-top condition.

Even so, Rooster Booster was again made a warm favourite. With the gallant mare Solerina ensuring a cracking pace, the race turned into as thrilling a hurdle race as can be imagined.

Conor O'Dwyer, loaned from Arthur Moore to be Hardy Eustace's regular jockey, joined the mare two out and pulled ahead turning into the straight. Rooster Booster did not miss the move and Richard Johnson had him challenging as they headed for the last. But in a thrilling run up to the line, it was the Irish hero who again proved himself best.

It was a deserved triumph for the trainer, whose career in racing nearly ended as a lad after a fall in Musselburgh, near Edinburgh, sidelined him for four months. He came home to Whitehall in Dublin, but a meeting with legendary Irish trainer Mick O'Toole got him restarted in 1968. Seven years later, he won the Cheltenham Gold Cup on Davy Lad, his first of nine winning rides there,

ending with Monksfield's Champion Hurdle in 1979.

The following year he took out a training licence, and on New Year's Day 1980 at Fairyhouse he rode his first winner as a trainer himself; he also trained Monksfield's first winning progeny, Black Monkey, for Countess Doenhoff.

'She was a lovely woman,' he remembers. 'Her father had been head of the German Jockey Club before Hitler took over.'

And his best moment in racing?

'It has to be training the Champion Hurdler.' Then he qualifies this a little. 'Well, riding was the more satisfying. With training, a lot of the time it is just a relief to win, so much is expected from the owners, and races are so difficult to win – but I do have very good owners now.'

No man could have deserved more to add training two Champion Hurdle winners to his riding of one.

WEXFORD

For Wexford, think Viking. Think sunny south-east. Think gateway to the rest of the world (and barely 20 minutes from Rosslare, where British visitors might arrive by ferry). And especially think friendly racecourse that top-class flat horses and jockeys attend, as well as a stream of NH ones.

This is a land within a land, the 'hidden island' invaded by Vikings, Normans and Danes. The area can lay claim to a cultural and heritage mixture of Gaelic, Anglo-Irish and Norman, and also the pretty town of Wexford, with its narrow streets, attractive quayside and world-famous annual opera.

The county has a hundred miles of coastline stretching up to the Wicklow Mountains in the north and as far south as Atlantic surf-swept Hook Head, with miles of sandy beaches, pretty coves and fishing villages, mountains, valleys, rivers Slaney and Barrow, holiday homes, spectacular scenery and rich agricultural land that is ideal for breeding thoroughbred horses. It is also the county where ace flat trainer Aidan O'Brien was born and reared, and plied his early trade.

Wexford was the newest Irish course of the twentieth century; only the new Limerick has come since, opened in 2001, exactly 50 years after Wexford. There are records of racing taking place on reclaimed bog land in the area in the 1870s, but this only continued until the turn of the century. If Wexford is a small course now, it was even smaller then, but nevertheless it drew 17,000 people to the opening, when admission prices were 10 shillings (50p/63c) for men, 5 shillings for ladies, and half a crown (12½p/20c) for access, excluding the enclosure. Seventy horses competed, each race being worth £130. The very first race, a two-mile handicap hurdle, was won by Hypernod, ridden by Jimmy Eddery, father of the famous Pat, 11 times champion flat jockey in Britain and once in Ireland (1992). On that

Aidan O'Brien and his 'right-hand man', his eldest son Joseph

afternoon two legendary Irish trainers also saddled winners, Dan Moore and Paddy 'Darkie' Prendergast.

In 1992, on 20 July, an Aga Khan-bred and owned filly by Lashkari called Sinntara won her maiden here for trainer John Oxx and jockey Johnny Murtagh. She had been knocking on the door with a third in Gowran and a fourth in Roscommon, but her Wexford win started her on a roll. She won her next three races on Ireland's major flat tracks of Leopardstown and The Curragh, including winning the Irish Cesarewitch that September. Once out in the paddocks as a brood mare, she produced dual Derby winner Sinndar, by Grand Lodge, for the same connections. A bay, like his dam, he had a lovely, equable temperament and he kept on improving. In eight runs he was only beaten once, by a short head. In 2000 he won the English and Irish Derbys and the Prix de l'Arc de Triomphe.

Sinntara's win at Wexford was one of the last before big renovations were undertaken at the track. The course had slipped into a poor condition and in 1987, encouraged by new managing director Michael Murphy, a supporters club was founded. The main aims were to raise funds to improve the condition of the track and to attract more people to the races. Initially the money was found from the supporters' own pockets. Through this and their various fundraising activities, they were able to level and drain the course and to camber the sharp bends. They also extended the track by an extra two furlongs.

This enthusiasm for the course by members of Wexford Supporters – more than 260 of them – was well rewarded, so much so that the club can now also afford to support local charities, including the Wexford Catscan Appeal, and to organise racing visits to Cheltenham and Chepstow.

The supporters have their own bar at Wexford, and they also sponsor annual Wexford awards, won in 2004 by three locals: trainer Paul Nolan, jockey Johnny Cullen and amateur rider N.P. Slippers Madden. Supporters club chairman Derek Nally says people join the club because 'They know a good thing when they see it!

'You get all sorts – people who are passionate about racing and people who wouldn't know one end of a horse from another. All are welcome.'

By 1993 the rewards for the supporters' work were felt through bigger fields, better racing and some top names. Indeed, the first race run on the realigned track was won by Mick Kinane just two days after he had won the Epsom Derby on Commander in Chief in June 1993.

But it is for NH that the course is best known and especially for its hunter chases, producing excellent trial races for the Cheltenham and Aintree Foxhunters, and Ireland's longest race, the La Touche at Punchestown. Names like Blunt's Cross,

Jumping at Wexford: Private Ben, A.D. Leigh up, trained by Jessica Harrington, and What A Native, ridden by A.P. Lane and trained by Charlie Swan

improve Wexford further, by extending the nine-furlong course by two and a half furlongs, thanks to the acquisition of a ten-acre block of land on a hill at the far end of the course. Its principal race of the year is the Listed People Newspapers Group Handicap Chase in October.

* * *

Driving down to Wexford on St Patrick's Day means passing several colourful parades along the way, a mood that is also apparent at the races. And they are so easy to find! At first I thought all the cars parked along the main road towards the town were for another parade, but no, there was the grandstand. The course looks over Wexford Harbour in the distance and is overlooked by houses and bungalows on two sides, giving a free view of the racing to any occupants should they feel inclined.

Today also coincides with the Cheltenham Festival, and Wexford uses a big screen for the first time, not only to display the day's racing, but also, in particular, to relay the day's races from over the water. People have come early and there is a good crowd; spring is in the air, with colourful daffodils, primulas and tulips in full flower around the single silver birch in the centre of the paddock. The trophy table is covered in the purple and yellow county colours. A kids' fun'n'games room frees up parents to enjoy the day's

who won here in 1961 on his way to La Touche victory and two years later the Galway Plate. Eliogarty won in 1983; his marvellous rider, Caroline Beasley, went on to be the first lady rider to win at Cheltenham, and then won at Aintree too. Lovely Citizen and Elegant Lord, one of owner J.P. McManus's favourite horses, won here prior to their Cheltenham Foxhunters victories of 1991 and 1996 respectively. In the late '60s, Noel Meade, Ireland's leading NH trainer, gained his only win as a rider here, in an amateur riders' hurdle in which he beat Dermot Weld and Mouse Morris on Tu Va.

Now there are more ambitious plans to

card of three hurdles, three chases and a bumper.

The most valuable race of the day is the hunter chase in which Bewleys Best is a popular winning favourite. Lillian Doyle from nearby Gorey trained him and Donal MacAulay rides. Breeder Gerald Foley presents the cup for the race, dating from 1952.

There is also a trophy for the handicap chase run in memory of Michael O'Murchadha, a founder of Wexford and father of the current managing director Michael Murphy – 'I found the Anglican spelling easier.'

His two young daughters, Anna and Mary, present the trophy to winning owner Derek Nally, who just happens to be chairman of Wexford Supporters (he also once stood as a candidate for President of Ireland). The winning horse, Vicars Way, trained locally by Pat Sinnott near Enniscorthy, is the first Derek Nally has ever owned, and this is his third win in a row: 'a dream come true'.

It was after a heart bypass operation in 1988 that his doctor told Derek it was time to start to relax. As general secretary of the Police Association and as president of the charity Victim Support this didn't come too easily.

'And I told him if he made me go hitting a little white ball, I'd be back for another bypass,' Derek Nally laughs, 'so I began going racing instead.'

The local flavour is much in evidence at

The paddock at Wexford. The course is just over one mile round, right-handed and fairly undulating

Presentation to the connections of Vicars Way, winner of the Michael O'Murchadha Handicap Chase

Wexford, none more so than with Chris O'Reilly, nearly 80 years old, who arrives at 9.30 in the morning with a rake over his shoulder ready to help out on the course.

'We can't stop him working,' Michael Murphy says. 'He's been part and parcel of this place since the beginning in 1952.'

Somehow, this is typical of the ethos of Wexford.

And, by the way, don't forget that if you visit Wexford in June, you can expect Ireland's first strawberries of the year, grown locally.

APRIL

FAIRYHOUSE

It is the week before 'the big one', the Irish Grand National at Fairyhouse – *Teach Na Scog*. Manager Dick Sheil is out walking the course with his prodding stick. Again.

It is something he does regularly throughout the year, and every day for a week before this race, sometimes twice in one day. Trainers ring constantly for updates on the going. The grass will be topped three times during the week to leave a thick 2-in. sward come race day; it is kept that way by foreman Noel Fanning and eight ground staff.

The Irish Grand National *is* Easter Monday to the Irish. Twenty thousand people are likely to flock through the turnstiles to bet on their fancies and witness the spectacle.

It is a race that lives up to its name for the fences are firm and big but beautifully presented and fair. They are there to be jumped. That is what steeplechasing is all about.

As we walk round the course, Dick Sheil gives me a running commentary: of which horse fell where in recent times; of how the track was laid out in bygone times; and of recent and proposed future developments to the buildings – the Jameson Stand was upgraded in 1989, the new Powers Stand opened in 1999, and plans for a new 15,000-metre-square hotel complex and entertainment centre set back from the home straight have been approved.

'We are only 13 miles from O'Connell Street in the centre of Dublin,' Dick Sheil points out.

We pass the river fence beside a stream that is a tributary of the River Tolka. The fences are 70 ft wide, of which 35–40 ft will be used on one race day, saving fresh ground for another day. Most of them are 4 ft 6 in. to 4 ft 8 in. high; the open ditch, or regulation, used to be 5 ft 2 in. high and 6 ft 8in. wide, but was reduced after concerns expressed by some jockeys, especially those who also ride in the UK on a regular basis.

At the end of 2004 and again in early 2005 the fences were modified further, and Dick Sheil believes they have now got them right.

Fairyhouse manager Dick Sheil and his prodding stick

The prodding stick, a stout piece of blackthorn given to Dick by course inspector and former crack amateur Billy McLernon when Dick took up this post in 1999, foretells a consistent good-to-yielding as we walk, until we reach the home straight where it is good. There, a line of three fences and a short 170-yard run-in await the runners. 'Some jockeys and trainers say it should be two fences and a longer run-in,' admits Dick.

But jumping is the name of the game. That and variety. Part of the charm of Irish and UK racing lies in the diversity of courses: shapes, sizes, undulations, flat, sharp, galloping, left- or right-handed.

That, apparently, is why the application for an all-weather track for Fairyhouse was turned down. Fairyhouse is right-handed; all American racing is uniformly left, and so the Americans wouldn't be likely to come.

But would they anyway? I thought the idea of a new all-weather track was to reduce the number of lower grade horses being balloted out here in Ireland . . .

* * *

It was back in the 1840s that a group of diehard followers of the Ward Union Hunt banded together and built the racetrack, forebears of the Leonard and Collen families foremost amongst them. These fearless horsemen of the renowned hard-riding carted-stag hunt have left their legacy not only in the course, but in their children and grandchildren too, who remain just as committed riding across country today. Crack Irish jockey Paul Carberry regularly whips in to this famous pack; no wonder it is so difficult to dislodge him from the saddle when a horse blunders. Another, Hugh Leonard, now in his 70s, won a chase in Fairyhouse and finished second in the La Touche at Punchestown in the 1950s, but in particular he recalls hacking a tiny 15.1hh black mare called Molly Brant the eight miles to Fairyhouse and back, two days running, because he had no transport. She was beaten by a neck in the Levins Moore Chase and was third there the following day in the Joseph O'Reilly Chase. She also won her first four point-to-points.

But it is the draining of the new course at Fairyhouse to which current users owe the founders an immense debt. For they dug the heavy loam to make drains four to five feet deep, and carried and laid by hand the stones for the drainage of the saucer-shaped bowl around which the track lies. 'It must have been backbreaking hard work,' remarks Dick Sheil, a former competitive cyclist who is not averse to hard work himself.

It was in 1870 that the Irish Grand National was first run, won by a horse called Sir Robert Peel over a distance of three miles two furlongs. In those days there was just this one day's racing a year, always on Easter Monday, which in 1916 coincided with the Easter Uprising (when the race was won by J. Kiernan's All Sorts;

the 1919 meeting was abandoned 'owing to the actions of Sinn Fein').

Today, there are 19 days' racing per year at the venue, and apart from the Easter Festival there is a popular two-day meeting in November. Even after the first race has been run, there are cars still queuing for a mile down the road waiting to get in.

Living up to the name of one of hurdling history's greats, the 2004 Hatton's Grace was won by the incredible mare Solerina from the aptly named Brave Inca in a performance that had the crowds cheering all the way from the last and again around the winner's enclosure, where they crammed six or seven deep.

In February the former Tom Dreaper Memorial Steeplechase, now the Bobbyjo, is run, and at the Easter meeting there is the Dan Moore Memorial two mile one furlong handicap chase. Hatton's Grace, Drinmore and Royal Bond are all remembered in December.

The Irish National meeting has been a three-day festival since 1972. The Sunday is 'family fun' day, when children are admitted free and there is children's entertainment throughout the day, plus a crèche, as well as an Easter Bunny competition and free Easter eggs for all. Monday is Irish Grand National day, which includes a best-dressed lady competition. It begins with previews and interviews of all the leading contenders for the big race by Gearoid Moynihan, who can be seen, microphone in hand, at many leading meetings throughout the year, smoothly coordinating the day's entertainment and prizegivings.

The Irish Grand National has been run over 3 miles 5 furlongs since 1976. It has been sponsored by the group that is now known as Irish Distillers, following the amalgamation between family Irish whiskey firms, Power and Jameson, since the 1960s. This firm is now the longest-running horse-race sponsor in the British Isles and Ireland following the demise of the Whitbread sponsorship in the UK. The good news for Irish whiskey drinkers and racegoers alike is that the firm has committed itself until at least 2014.

In 2004 a total of 450 horses ran over Easter, 168 of them on Grand National day.

Some of the greatest names of Irish racing have graced the winners' list and a few from the UK, too. One of the most amazing was a mare called Alike in 1929 whose jockey, Frank Wise, had a wooden leg, was missing three fingers and was also very short.

From 1876 to 1880 the race was dominated by the riding Beasley brothers, Tommy, Johnny and Harry. Tommy won it on Grand National and Thiggin Thue, Johnny on Juggler and Harry on Controller. All three of them and a fourth brother, Willie, rode in the 1879 Aintree Grand National, and it is Harry's grandson, Bobby, who won that race on Nicolaus Silver in 1961 and the Cheltenham Gold Cup on Captain Christy in 1974, bringing many a tear to Irish eyes.

Ireland's Prime Minister, An Taoiseach Bertie Ahern, presenting the Tom Dreaper Perpetual Trophy to Martin Brassil, the trainer of Numbersixvalverde, winner of the 2005 Powers Gold Label Irish Grand National

The 1904 Irish Grand National winner, Ascetic's Silver, won the Aintree version two years later, having dislodged his jockey at the third in the intervening year. Ascetic's Silver, like Cloister and Drumcree, two other Aintree Grand

National winners, was sired by Ascetic, a horse so useless on the racecourse that he was used to collect post. Such are the vagaries of breeding. And the reason why so many continue to breed. In the hope theirs might be the next 'big one', the next Arkle or Best Mate.

There have only been a handful of English-trained winners of the Irish Grand National. The first was Rhyme 'N Reason in 1985, followed five years later by the popular English hero Desert Orchid, who powered his grey frame to victory in 1990. The 2004 winner, Granit d'Estruval, was trained in Yorkshire by Irishman Ferdy Murphy and ridden by Corkman Brian Harding, it being his first jumping victory in his native land.

Brian grew up in Castletownroche, where both his parents rode in point-to-points and now train them, as does his sister, Maria, who is also a talented chef. Brian himself was a regular on the pony-racing scene. He was then apprenticed to Kevin Prendergast before moving to England. He is best remembered, still as a young fellow, for his winning ride on the stunning grey One Man in the Queen Mother Champion Chase, only for the horse to be killed under him a fortnight later over the Mildmay course at Aintree.

* * *

Back to the Irish National, one name dominates the list: Dreaper, father and son. Tom Dreaper trained ten different winners, beginning with Prince Regent, carrying 12 st. 7 lb, in 1942; Shagreen, 10 st. 10 lb, in 1949; and Royal Approach, 12 st., in 1954. Then his winning sequence extended to an amazing seven years in a row, beginning with Olympia, carrying 9 st. 11 lb, in 1960; Fortria, 12 st.; Kerforo, 10 st. 3 lb; Last Link, 9 st. 7 lb; Arkle, 12 st.; Splash, 10 st. 13 lb; and Flying Bolt, 12 st. 7 lb, a truly amazing feat, especially with horses whose weights ranged from a mere 9 st. 7 lb to a mighty 12 st. 7 lb.

After Tom Dreaper's retirement, his son, Jim, trained the winner four times, once with Colebridge and three times with Brown Lad.

Brown Lad's wins were amazing; only two other horses in the race's history have won it twice, and they were back in the early years: Scots Grey ridden by Mr Garrett Moore in 1872 and 1875, and The Gift ridden by T. Kelly in 1883 and 1884.

It is a race that over the years has captured the imagination of Irish racegoers and is a must in many laypeople's diary every year. They don't go away disappointed.

* * *

For the six or seven years that Arkle was in his heyday, Jim Dreaper was in boarding school, and when he was home for the summer holidays, Arkle was away on his owner's farm for his. It was impossible, of course, for the impact of such a great horse not to have rubbed off on the young Jim. It was the third decade in which his father, Tom, ruled supreme in the Irish NH training world. Anne, Duchess of Westminster's Arkle remains to most NH fans *the* greatest, but imagine training a horse of the calibre of Flyingbolt as a number two.

The wishy-washy chestnut with a broad white face was bred in England by Mr R.E. Way and sold as a foal to Fidelma Harty in Patrickswell, Co. Limerick; re-sold as a yearling to Major George Ponsonby in Co. Tipperary, where he was broken, and was bought for racing by Mrs T.G. Wilkinson. From the start, Flyingbolt lived up to his name and after winning his bumper first time out in 1963 under top amateur Alan Lillingston (who had won the Champion Hurdle earlier the same year on Winning Fair), he remained unbeaten in Ireland for nearly two years. In 1965 he won the Cotswold Chase and the Massey Ferguson Gold Cup at Cheltenham, and the Black and White Gold Cup at Ascot. The next spring he not only won the two-mile Champion Chase (now the Queen Mother) at Cheltenham, but also finished third in the Champion Hurdle the very next day. Only a month later he humped 12 st. 7 lb to win the Irish National, ridden as usual by Pat Taaffe. Sadly, Flyingbolt succumbed to a blood disease and was never the same again.

As for the Irish Grand National, Tom

Arkle in box number seven at Greenogue with trainer Tom Dreaper, daughter Valerie and Sputnik the terrier

Dreaper, as we have seen, made it his own, starting in 1942 with Prince Regent, the great horse that also won the Cheltenham Gold Cup in 1946 and was third and fourth in the Grand National under huge weights. We can only imagine how much more he might have won had it not been for the war years. Tom considered Prince Regent the greater horse for many of Arkle's early years.

Tom Dreaper grew up in a well-known Co. Meath farming family, close to their current home of Greenogue, Killsullaghan, that is little changed today, filled with pictures of winners, hunting portraits, and all the paraphernalia of family country life steeped in farming, hunting and NH

racing. He was 48 when he married Elizabeth 'Betty' Russell, and three children, Eva (married to now retired flat trainer Michael Kauntze), Jim and Valerie, followed.

Tom was first and foremost a cattle and hunting man for whom point-to-pointing and training became a natural progression. A cattle dealer of repute, he was also a dashing follower of the Ward Union Staghounds, and winning the Hunt Cup each year at the local point-to-point was his goal. Tom won it and he won as an amateur under Rules, as son Jim and grandson Tom have done since. The training was a more serious job – in those days, the trainer was very much the servant of the owner; there was no percentage of the purse or special trainer's prize.

At the time that Tom was training, most of the good horses bred in Ireland were snapped up by English owners to be trained there. It led to a dearth of good racing in Ireland, a similar position to that which New Zealand has found itself in latterly, with most of its good bloodstock sold to run abroad. It meant that Irish races could be cherry-picked with those few good horses that were left, and Tom was in the fortunate position of having good owners who, though many were English, were willing to keep their horses with him. Number one among these was Lord Bicester, whose Royal Approach won the 1954 Irish Grand National as a novice six year old, carrying 12 st. There were also

Colonel Sir John Thomson, J.V. Rank, a number of other bankers and Anne, Duchess of Westminster, who, as Nancy Sullivan, had grown up in Co. Cork. The other Irish trainers who shared the bulk of the wealthy NH owners were Paddy Sleator, Dan Moore, Willie O'Grady and Phonsie O'Brien, but not Vincent O'Brien, who had already turned his talented hand to the Flat. Nowadays there are plenty of wealthy Irish owners and the standard of the sport has never been healthier.

Jim always planned to train, though it probably came sooner than expected – aged 19, his father became ill and had to retire. At the time Jim was an aspiring amateur rider and had finished second to Specify in the Aintree Grand National on Black Secret in 1971.

Jim takes up the story: 'I walked the course with Sean Barker, who was riding Vulture, and Pat Black, Gay Buccaneer. When we looked at the first, I wondered what all the fuss was about, but about 50 yards from the third we could see a tractor and trailer in the ditch between the guard-rail and the fence. Pat Black said, "I've seen enough" and turned back. In the race he made the running until a loose horse knocked him over at the Canal Turn first time round.

'I still didn't feel too daunted until I was in the weighing room with all the legends – Stan Mellor, Terry Biddlecombe, and so on. There was the traditional speech along the lines of "It's a long race, take your time." There was a total change of atmosphere from that moment; it was like flicking a switch and getting serious.

'During the next half-hour there were a number of places I would have liked to have been, and the weighing room at Aintree wasn't one of them. This feeling continued all the way to the start; everything seemed wrong, and the preliminaries seemed to go on forever.

'It was fine once we started. I was in mid-division approaching the Chair and ten strides out I had a perfect view, and at five, but then some other horses pulled across me and I couldn't see it, but the horse jumped it perfectly. The only mistake Black Secret made was at the 23rd, which had a hole in it. I lost a stirrup and hung on for five strides.'

From there on Black Secret just kept going better and better so that he led over the last fence and then suffered the nightmare of that long, long run in and failed by just a neck to last home.

It was a wonder Black Secret ever raced at all, let alone so well in the world's most famous race. Owned by Jim's godmother, Carol Watney, he had been bought as a yearling by Tom Dreaper, but at three was 'a wrong 'un'; he was gone in the wind (a breathing defect), suffered from splints (bony growths on the lower forelegs) and curbs (ditto of the hind legs) and to cap it all had a 'McEnroe' temperament. Sean Barker 'went through hell with him,' Jim

says. 'The horse would do nothing willingly except eat.'

He rode him in the afternoons, when the rest of the horses and lads would be having a rest, and tried to knock it out of him jumping all sorts of obstacles along the way. Hunting, as with many a temperamental horse, was the making of him, and Sean was to be rewarded for his efforts when riding him into third place in the 1972 Grand National, won by Well To Do.

Before that Jim won a couple of point-to-points on him. He was unseated from him in a hunter chase in Fairyhouse, so rather than repeat that exercise in Punchestown he ran him in a bumper and finished third. He won a couple of races but was no world-beater, though he was an excellent jumper.

Jim recalls finishing third on him in the Kim Muir Chase for amateur riders at the Cheltenham Festival. The winner was Michael Dickinson on Rainbow Valley with Colonel Piers Bengough, a true Corinthian who died in April 2005, second.

'My lasting memory,' says Jim, 'is of sharing the lead with the colonel at the top of the final hill where Michael swept past both of us on the corner and then pulled in sharply in front of us.

'The colonel was riding long and sporting his moustache as usual, and as we gathered ourselves together he called out, "I say!" No swearing, but Michael had gone ten minutes anyway . . .'

* * *

One of the many things Jim learnt from his father was in caring for horses' legs. Tom could be said to have been one of the first 'interval' trainers long before that term was coined, and he also had a quick mathematical mind. He used to tell Jim to count the number of strides a horse took over 100 yards, and then ask him how many it would be if the stride was shortened by 20 per cent. Nearly always, if a horse has been fired (an operation to try and strengthen a tendon after a horse has broken down), the stride will be that much shorter. A quick horse will seldom be as good again because that little bit of stretch has gone.

Jim enjoyed a magical decade when he first took over the licence and himself trained the winner of the Irish Grand National four times, beginning with Colebridge in 1974, a horse out of Arkle's sister, for owner Mrs P. Burrell. For the next two runnings the race was won by the same owner's Brown Lad, and again in 1978.

Brown Lad was bred by Joe Osborne and came to Jim having already won a novice hurdle at Cheltenham. 'He was big, plain, pigeon-toed and very lethargic at home; if anything finished behind him on the gallops, we thought that horse must be either lame or dead. As for jumping schooling fences, Brown Lad just wouldn't have a go, even though he'd been a good hurdler. We wondered what we were doing wrong with him, but Tommy Carberry scrambled through a couple of chases with

him and he was allotted a low weight in the Irish Grand National; he won it, and again the next year, carrying 12 st. 2 lb, then he missed a year. When he won it for a third time, Tommy Carberry chose to ride something else and Gerry Dowd, a claimer in our yard, rode him, they just got on together.

'Brown Lad was one of the better horses in the last half century who did not win a Cheltenham Gold Cup. He needed it heavy, as it was the year that it snowed and the race was postponed until April, by which time it was good-to-firm.' That was in 1978. Brown Lad was second to Midnight Court and his stable companion, Colebridge, was third.

Jim Dreaper had won a Gold Cup, however, with Anne, Duchess of Westminster's Ten Up in 1975, who, like Brown Lad, was also bred by Joe Osborne.

Joe is remembered as a fearless rider, trainer, breeder and producer from the 1920s. Three times he won the Kildare Hunt Cup over four miles, with the mare Alice Whitethorn carrying 13 st. 3 lb on the last occasion. She became dam of Irish National winner Alice Maythorn, and her own dam, Alice Rockthorn, won the Galway Plate of 1914.

Today Jim has a number of nice, quality horses in his yard and one of them is a French-bred horse named Jim. Owned by Pat Conway, he was named before arriving at Jim Dreaper's yard, where he was nicknamed Jiminy.

Jim Dreaper, carrying on the Greenogue tradition

'Well, he was disappointing at first, and I didn't want to hear lads saying, "That Jim is f***ing useless,"' Jim reasons.

Jiminy has improved since those days, though is but an apprentice compared with the stars of the past –'but he tries hard and jumps well,' says Jim. A fall when leading at Navan in March 2004 saw about five horses land on him and he came back with a dozen bleeding wounds. He was not himself that autumn and so it was especially good to see him win a nice race, the Micky Holly Memorial Chase at Leopardstown, in March 2005.

Jim Dreaper and his delightful wife Tricia also have the pleasure of watching their son, Tom, riding with success as an amateur in England.

SLIGO

Sligo is Yeats country. The Irish have centuries, millennia, as literary people. Racing is but a young pup to storytelling and reading. Put the two together and you have Sligo, way off in the north-west of Ireland.

The racecourse is on the outskirts of Sligo town, and on a clear day it is easy to see where the Yeats brothers' inspiration came from, William Butler with his poems and Jack Butler, the more likely to be seen at a race meeting, with his expressive paintings of racehorses, as well as of horse fairs, and general Irish country life and current affairs. Jack also wrote, and William, who is buried at Drumcliff, Co. Sligo, had begun life wanting to be an artist; their father was both.

The peaks of Benbulben and Knocknarea stand erect each side of Sligo town, and then not far away is Innisfree – 'I shall arise and go now . . .'

Lisadell, the stately Sligo home of Irish nationalist and Easter Rising rebel Constance Markievicz, is one of the places where William Butler Yeats used to stay. Slish Wood, Drumcliffe, Hazelwood, Dooney – these are surrounding places that inspired both the poet and the artist.

Sligo county can also boast some of the most important prehistoric monuments in Ireland. There is a megalithic burial site near the town and another in the mountains. The grave of Queen Maeve of Connaught is said to be in the county and her cairn on Knocknarea Mountain is meant to be over 40 ft high; but then legends and folklore go hand in hand with the beauty and aura of the county's lakes, islands and mountains.

Racing is known to have taken place in the Sligo area since 1781, when there were meetings at Bowmore on Rosses Point, a name that is familiar to listeners of the Irish shipping forecast. Racing in the nineteenth century was already so popular nationwide that by 1814 the organising committee of Sligo races decided to 'commence its meeting in August so as to give the racehorses time to travel to Bellewstown, Maze, Derry and Monaghan, and to come to Sligo'. In 1893 the local newspaper recorded that 'the beauty and fashion of the county attended the races'.

There followed a difficult period when the races were at times stopped due to political turmoil and faction fighting. The course moved to Hazelwood from 1898 until 1942 when it ceased altogether until the current site at Cleveragh on the edge of the town was opened in 1955.

Sligo holds seven meetings each summer, from late April until mid-August, six evenings and one Sunday afternoon, at which it features the Guinness Handicap Hurdle, a trial for the Galway Hurdle. Its feature race used to be the Connacht National, but steeplechasing ceased on the track about ten years ago. However, if the chasing is restored, its national would be back too. Meanwhile, to celebrate 50 years at its current site, a €30,000 hurdle was held in 2005.

Sligo may be in the far west, but it has become accessible for visitors via its airport at Strandhill, only six miles away, and the well-used pilgrimage airport at Knock, thirty-five miles distant. For those combining racing with holidaymaking, there is fishing, golf and riding, as well as several beaches, some of which have gained a good reputation for surfing.

Benbulben didn't deign to show itself on my visit to the racecourse, but the track itself was welcoming and it was easy to see the whole course, set in probably the smallest acreage of all the Irish racecourses.

It's a course at which a horse or trainer can find a happy hunting ground, and one trainer who fits that bill is James Burns, son of legendary jockey/trainer Thomas – T.P. – Burns. James has regularly made the long journey from The Curragh worthwhile and has become one of the leading flat trainers on the track as a result. On my visit the three flat races were held first, and the James Burns-trained Rochetto, a winner on this course in June, can only finish fourth this time, two lengths behind Edward Lynham's charge, Badger Kennedy, ridden by Declan McDonogh, son of trainer Des McDonogh, who will always be remembered for his marvellous handling of dual champion hurdler Monksfield.

It is a murky, damp August evening

James Burns, the Curragh-based trainer with a good record at Sligo, a small course on the edge of the town

–'Come earlier in the summer,' James Burns had advised – but it is brightened for those with sharp eyes by an emerging star when Jazz Princess makes her racecourse debut over seven furlongs. Ridden by Pat Cosgrove for trainer Jessica Harrington, she beats the nearest of her thirteen opponents by one and a half lengths at a price of 10–1. She followed this up by accounting for 14 rivals over a mile at Galway in September, and then scored a splendid three out of three for joint owners T. Curran and M.O. Cullinane with a win in a Group 3 race at The Curragh in October before going into 'winter quarters' unbeaten – and she had cost only €9,000 at public auction.

It was back in April 2002 on heavy

ground that Sligo was again chosen as a suitable venue for a future star to make its racing debut, and that was Brewster, now a crack hurdler in England and likely to be even better over fences. Back on that April evening he was ridden to win the bumper by Ulsterman Peter Buchanan, an amateur at the time, but now riding professionally from a base in Scotland.

The late Terry Casey, former jockey and trainer of 1996 Grand National winner Rough Quest when he was based in England, is remembered at Sligo. A native of Donegal, he spent much of his working life in Co. Monaghan before heading for the English Midlands where he rode subsequent Grand National winner, Grittar, to his first two hurdling victories. Terry then turned to training, which culminated with the win of Rough Quest in the Aintree Grand National, before illness shortened his career. Terry is no longer alive, but that he is not forgotten was shown by six Irish friends, headed by Colm Herron of the Hill Grove Hotel in Monaghan, who sponsor a race in his name at Sligo, the nearest course to his childhood home. In August 2005 the Terry Casey Memorial Hurdle was won by a filly called No Sound, steered to a clear victory by Denis O'Regan for Noel Meade.

Trainer Billy Boyers had not one acre of land, yet he sent out a steady stream of winners from his Sligo base, not just within Ireland but also to Scotland, and to

Jazz Princess inaugurated her hat-trick at Sligo and then the following year went on to be Jessica Harrington's first runner in a Classic

the Cheltenham Festival, no less (his horse Kilcoleman triumphed in the County Hurdle). He also won a Galway Plate in 1980 with Sir Barry and trained the winner of the Connaught National four times.

He might have had no land, but he was able to use the strand known as the second beach at Rosses Point to great effect (just as the great Red Rum had on Southport sands in England). There is nothing like sea water for horses' legs.

Boyers also provided Enda Bolger's first winner as he was feeling his way into the jumping game, on a horse called Tieragh

Enda Bolger (left), seen here receiving a trophy at Limerick,
rode his first winner for Sligo trainer Billy Boyers

Prince in a bumper at Kilbeggan. No other feeling quite like it, the first win.

'He was a lovely man,' says Enda. 'Sligo was a long way away, yet he would have winners at Leopardstown, and I rode some winners for him at Ayr. It was easy to take the ferry from Belfast to Stranraer.' It was on that course that Enda beat the then leading jockey, Ron Barry, in a handicap chase. 'He seemed like God,' Enda recalls.

Billy Boyers was applauded by his home county in 2004 when he was inducted into the Hall of Fame at the *Sligo Weekender* Sports Awards, covering many different sports, with the words, 'Billy Boyers, for so long the cornerstone of horse racing in the north-west.'

A genuinely surprised Billy Boyers said that he 'might have started out with donkeys', but he liked to think that Kilcoleman and Sir Barry were his star performers in a different league.

MAY

PUNCHESTOWN

Punchestown represents a microcosm for the whole of Irish racing, where generations of families have left their indelible mark on this wonderful piece of Co. Kildare countryside. Legends, dynasties, names like Mullins, Dreaper and Osborne, Flood, Cox and Doyle, Molony, Hyde, Taaffe and O'Grady, Moore and Walsh, Weld, Prendergast and Sleator, and Hogan and Harty. Legends all, sometimes over two or three generations. Many of them rode when Punchestown races were run over banks and walls, pre-1960.

Punchestown is Ireland's own-brand answer to Cheltenham. Its four-day festival at the end of April, sometimes spilling into early May, brings together the champions of Cheltenham, Aintree, Fairyhouse and, these days, from France too, for the final deciding round of the season. It is a beautiful location and an excellent, testing course of two miles round, and visitors from all the countries concerned flock through its modernised turnstiles to enjoy the festival flavour and championship-class racing.

First and foremost it was originally the course for the local hunt, the Kildare, to stage its annual meetings; the fox is part of Punchestown's logo too. The hunt had used a number of locations until plumping for Punchestown as its permanent venue in 1850. The first known meeting was in 1824 over two days, followed three years

Running across country, Punchestown, Co. Kildare

later by a four-day meeting, and in 1828 with a five-day programme. The Kildare Hunt Cup was founded in 1837 as a two-mile race 'over a sporting country'. At that time races were still run in heats with a final, but in 1842 the Kildare broke new ground by running the cup as a single race.

It was in 1854 that Punchestown became a two-day meeting on its permanent course, with races over banks and walls, and so it remained for the next hundred years. It was only in 1960 that steeplechase races over birch fences were included, followed by hurdle races a year later. In due course both bumper races and flat races were added.

Today there is another dimension. Looking out over the large track the viewer will see all sorts of strange-looking obstacles in the in-field: miniature castle, thatched roofs, a variety of timber constructions, archways and ponds with logs either side of them. All of these are the sort of fences that make up the cross-country phase of a three-day event. In the distance on the far side of the course are huge earthworks marking yet another quarry that is a trademark of a blossoming economy.

Punchestown has also become the National Centre for Equestrian and Field Sports of Ireland. Inside the huge, 60,000-foot-square structure it can house 2,000 smart tables during the racing festival, or be home to a variety of exhibitions, or take 80,000 fans for a pop concert, or can equally be turned into a trot-up point and veterinary inspection unit for horses, as it was during the World Endurance Championships of 2003.

All that is a far cry from the days when the cavalry and infantry personnel used to erect an acre of tented village here to host their friends to free lunch. In the end this became so abused that it was stopped (so what's new . . .). The military played a large part in the early days of Punchestown, as they did at other courses of the time, with some true Corinthian jockeys and many heroic tales. The Corinthian Cup at Punchestown was the forerunner of the Conyingham Cup founded in 1865 and run over four miles.

It is no surprise that future Aintree Grand National winners often ran their trials in the

cup, and among those who won this race to go on to Aintree glory are Seaman, Frigate, Come Away and Lovely Cottage.

When the National Hunt Chase was introduced in 1861 its £300 purse, added to a £5 sweepstake, made it the most valuable race in Ireland. Racing was thriving. Punchestown built permanent stands and laid out enclosures, and the attractive card remained much the same for the next century.

The introduction of chases and hurdles in the early 1960s resulted in an immediate upgrade in the class of horse running. A perfect example is the Martin Mahony Champion Novice Hurdle of 1961, the inaugural year of hurdles. There were nineteen runners, two of whom fell. The horse that finished fourth was Anzio, one of the first of the now regular English raiders, trained by Fulke Walwyn and ridden by the incomparable Fred Winter. The combination went on to win the following year's Champion Hurdle at Cheltenham. Yet one of the two fallers was even more interesting. His rider, Dave Dick, said that in spite of the fall 'someone should snap him up'. The horse was Mill House, winner of the 1963 Cheltenham Gold Cup and the 1967 Whitbread Gold Cup. In the intervening years he was usurped by none other than Arkle, 'Himself'.

In 1963 Punchestown became a three-day meeting and, faced with only two opponents, Arkle cakewalked the John Jameson Cup.

Jumpers in action at Punchestown

Some of the banks races survive today, adding to Punchestown's unique atmosphere, though they were somewhat emasculated in 2004 when the organisers were faced with either filling in the ditches on the grounds of safety or losing the races. They opted for the former; the meeting would certainly be the poorer without them.

The La Touche Cup is named after Percy La Touche, manager at Punchestown from 1892 until his death in 1921. A steward both of the Flat and National Hunt authorities, a colleague described him as 'a great Irishman, a good sportsman and the most outstanding personality in the world of sport of his generation'.

He was known for the work he did as a turf authority and legislator, and he also rode and won at Punchestown himself, in a private match against the Master of the

Jumping the famous double bank then (1960s) and today (2000s)

Kildare Hunt, Sir John Kennedy. The race named after him has been run since the early 1900s. It is a race in which two men and one horse have outstanding records – P.P. Hogan, Enda Bolger and Risk Of Thunder.

* * *

A strand of barbed wire stretches taut some 3 ft in front of an awesome hedge. One horse and rider, and one alone, clear it as if it's a run-of-the-mill obstacle. No one else even attempts it.

It is the Co. Limerick foxhounds, and the rider in question is Enda Bolger. Some horseman. No wonder he made the La Touche Cup his own. His and Risk Of Thunder's, that is.

Hard-mouthed, crooked-legged, pigeon-toed, pinfired and gone in the wind; that was Risk Of Thunder. He also possessed 'the longest ears ever seen on a horse'. Have a look next time he parades. A real character, he loved nothing more than to roll the moment his box was mucked out, sometimes barely waiting for the new straw to go down.

He won thirteen races, all bar one of them at Punchestown where he became a great public favourite over the banks, and where Enda Bolger was unbeaten on him in five memorable rides. Enda retired after his last win on Risk Of Thunder in April 1999, but had been a trainer since 1986, so the horse continued under his care and was particularly unlucky not to win the Velka Pardubice, the Czech Grand National over a diverse cross-country course. The popular

horse also made his finale a winning one at Punchestown three years later.

Risk Of Thunder was originally bought by Neilus Hayes, whose wife, Noreen, trained him under permit to win his first four banks races in Punchestown. Enter actor Sean Connery. He admitted he would love a made horse. Risk Of Thunder was not for sale, but since Enda had twice finished second to him, unable to get in a blow, he suggested they try and buy him. Eventually a deal was agreed – 'One of the best things I have ever done,' says Enda, who then trained and often rode him for new owners Sean Connery, J.P. McManus, John Magnier and Dermot Desmond. Risk Of Thunder now leads 'the life of a king', turned out with Istabraq in Martinstown, Co. Tipperary.

Risk Of Thunder, 'The Boss', won 12 races at Punchestown

As a lad in Co. Kilkenny, Enda Bolger helped at Paddy Mullins's stables before being employed there – 'a bit too young to take in just how good he was', Enda comments. From there, he moved to P.P. Pat Hogan first and then to Billy Boyers in Sligo, for whom he rode his first winners. But it was a call back to ride for P.P. Hogan that set him on course for 15 years with him. At first he declined to ride over banks, having had many falls schooling over them at home, but once he started, he caught the buzz. He went on to be a great trainer of banks horses – his latest star being Spot Thedifference – from his model Bruree base in Co. Tipperary.

When the Punchestown banks races looked in jeopardy in 2004, it was Enda Bolger who came up with the idea of filling the ditches on one or both sides of some of the banks with sand, which at least was startling enough for the horses to make them jump.

'The La Touche course is a piece of cake now,' says Enda, 'but the powers that be were getting a lot of stick from the safety authorities.'

* * *

For many people, spectators and those involved in racing alike, Punchestown is their favourite course. One trainer has a double reason for it being so.

When Jessica Harrington rode in the European Championships at Punchestown in 1967, she can little have guessed that thirty years on she would be winning there as trainer of some of Ireland's best steeplechasers and hurdlers. No wonder the glorious expanse of mature turf in the heart of Co. Kildare has become a spiritual second home to her.

Growing up with her older brother, John Fowler, in a sporting country home – their father, Brigadier Friz Fowler, was Master of the Meath Hunt, a Phoenix Park polo player and a keen point-to-point man – it was expected of Jessica that she would go down the eventing route, leaving the racing to her brother.

So it may have remained. Her eventing included three wins at Punchestown, four visits to Badminton with an impressive best-placed third, and she represented her country in European and World championships and the substitute Olympics (the year Moscow was boycotted), many of these on a home-bred mare called Amoy. She remains the last Irish rider to have won a three-star event at Punchestown when she triumphed in the late 1980s.

Her father had a permit and also bred thoroughbreds, and it was on one of them that she rode in her only point-to-point, finishing second, before the ride went back to her brother, now a successful trainer who won some 450 point-to-points and races under Rules as an amateur rider.

It was after her second marriage (the first to an English farmer in the Heythrop Hunt produced James and Tara) to John Harrington in Moone in Co. Kildare, close to the Wicklow Mountains, that training entered her life. First she had two more children – Emma, then Kate, who is still at school and 'keeps me young', laughs Jessica.

Moone is a tiny village steeped in history. It has a thriving Cistercian Monastery whose monks run a big dairy farm; they also say Mass if the parish priest is away and will conduct weddings, confirmations and so on. There is a well-preserved High Cross and several ruined castles. In the grounds of the Harringtons' home, Commonstown, is a plaque marking where there used to be an ancient chapel.

John Harrington bred thoroughbreds and had a permit to train, and also worked for the Curragh Bloodstock Agency. This took him away a lot and so Jessica took over the permit, training her first winner in 1987. Not long after, the couple found themselves with a number of unsold fillies (many will recognise the problem), so to take out a public licence, whereby she could train for non-family owners, seemed the solution.

Jessica began with just five horses. That was in 1989. Only a few years later, she had become a household name in racing circles on both sides of the Irish Sea. Her first winner, Lady Olean, was ridden for her by Peter Scudamore in a juvenile hurdle in Leopardstown.

'She was just short of top class but could win at the Grade 1 tracks,' Jessica recalls. Others soon followed: Brockley Court; Oh So Grumpy, who won the Galway Plate in 1994; the novice chase at the Punchestown Festival, now known as the Swordlestown Cup; as well as chases at Ascot and Kempton. Dance Beat and the home-bred Space Trucker followed.

Space Trucker ran 66 times, both flat and jumping, winning a total of 15 races. He proved a horse out of the top drawer, finishing third in the Champion Hurdle to Make a Stand and winning the Grand Annual Handicap Steeplechase, the oldest race in the calendar, also at Cheltenham. Space Trucker had fallen in his previous chase, and his chasing handicap was 2 st. inferior to his hurdling one. There were 15 runners and jockey Shay Barry, riding at 10 st. 1 lb, was told in no uncertain terms, 'Whatever you do, don't appear until after the last fence.' And that's exactly what he did.

'He gave him a brilliant ride,' says Jessica, 'and it was both his first win at Cheltenham and mine.'

Dance Beat was a lovely little mare who won the Ladbroke Hurdle at Leopardstown, but sadly was killed at Punchestown the same day that Space Trucker won a hurdle race in Cheltenham. John Harrington was at the English meeting and Jessica was with Dance Beat.

Jessica is good with mares and another one she reserves special affection for is Spirit Leader. 'She was amazing. She finished second in seven hurdles, but in hindsight they were good horses beating her.'

Spirit Leader then won three top English handicap hurdles, a prestigious trio that has never been emulated, beginning with the William Hill at Sandown in December, carrying 10 st., followed by the Tote Gold Trophy (the former Schweppes) at Newbury in February and culminating in the County Hurdle at the Cheltenham Festival in spite of her weight having gone up to a whopping 11 st. 6 lb.

That was the beginning of an incredible few days for Jessica, who in the same week won the Queen Mother Champion Chase with Moscow Flyer and the Midlands Grand National with Intelligent, giving jockey Robert Power his first English win.

Spirit Leader was sold for £156,000 at Doncaster Bloodstock Sales, in foal to Exit to Nowhere. 'Her new owner lives near us in Athy, so I hope we'll get some of her produce to train in due course,' says Jessica.

It was yet another mare trained by Jessica who gave Barry Geraghty his first win in England on Miss Orchestra, back in 1998, in the Midlands Grand National at Uttoxeter.

'He was 17 years old and hadn't yet lost all of his claim. He rode her at 9 st. 9 lb. She shied at a pram on the way to the start and dropped him; I didn't see it but he was big enough to tell me.' This is another mare that has now gone to stud, for comedian Jethro, and is also in foal to Exit to Nowhere.

And then along came Moscow.

Moscow Flyer, bay gelding by Moscow Society standing just 16 hands high. Bought unbroken at the Tattersalls (Ireland) Derby Sales for rookie owner Brian Kearney, newly retired civil engineer. 'Don't just play golf, get a new interest,' his racing loving son Conor cajoled.

Price limit twenty thousand. Small horse, unfashionable breeding and near the end of the sale. But lovely natural balance. 'Every time he walked out of the box he looked well balanced. Good third-generation pedigree, but nothing much closer. Bred to be a staying chaser.'

Bought for a meagre 17,000 Irish guineas. Couldn't win a bumper in four attempts. Seemed very slow. Summer holiday. Strengthened up, matured – and transformation. Record now is twenty-six wins, three seconds, three thirds from forty-one starts.

Was a good enough hurdler to be a champion, but what might have been 'his' year was lost to foot-and-mouth. Met Istabraq three times, each time one of them fell, leaving victory to the other. Never once did they fight out a finish together.

Then to chasing. His extraordinary record reads: fell, three wins, fell, three wins, unseated rider, three wins, unseated rider, three wins, unseated rider, six wins, up to his memorable second Queen Mother in March

Moscow Flyer on summer holiday after rolling in the mud

2005. Another brilliant win at Aintree, possibly his most impressive, after that, giving Barry Geraghty a dream ride, and on to Punchestown at the season's finale where the finish was so tight that the judge had to scrutinise the photo for several minutes. By the closest of margins, a short head, Moscow Flyer had been beaten by Rathgar Beau.

'He had to be beaten one day,' said Jessica, 'it was almost a relief.'

As a trainer, Jessica Harrington is one of the tops – she trained four Grade 1 winners in the first few weeks of 2005, two of them with new Champion Hurdle favourite Macs Joy, plus the Arkle Chase at Leopardstown with Ulaan Baatar, and the P.J. Moriarty Memorial Chase at the next Leopardstown meeting with Carrigeen Victor.

'Is that the opposition now?' Moscow Flyer sizes up the cattle

Jessica Harrington is full of praise for the way Irish racing is going. 'The government puts a lot of money in, prize money is good with a minimum value, plus there are grants for course facilities, such as drainage, track widening, new stands, new stables and so on. So long as we can keep people coming racing and the standard remains high, it will continue to thrive.

'I'm a great supporter of racing syndicates; they bring in new owners from all walks of life, who on their own would not be able to afford to keep and run a racehorse. They bring their friends and families racing – and usually they wouldn't dream of selling their horse.'

As a person, she is one of the tops, too, aided by husband Johnny, family, assorted dogs, helper Breda (with her for 30 years) and loyal stable staff, headed by Eamon Leigh, also there for 30 years. Wearing a smart shirt, collar and tie, he turns himself out as immaculately as he does 'his' horse for the races. He took over caring for Moscow Flyer after a number of staff left, but even a man of his experience had to have his wits about him when the horse was fit. 'Yes, he did buck me off and I broke my wrist once in the early days,' he recalls. But he is never far from the star's side, for even in the summer it is to Eamon's field that Moscow Flyer repairs for his well-earned holiday.

'That's when we both take our shoes off and relax,' Eamon says, adding, 'He'll tell us when he's ready to retire.'

Barry Geraghty, seen here at Kilbeggan, has won 25 races on Moscow Flyer

79

BALLINROBE

There is a warmth about Ballinrobe that may be because the runners are never far away. They can be seen easily from the stands throughout a race as they sweep along the undulating, almost park-like, tree-studded backstretch and then swing right-handed for home, the whole circuit being only a fraction over one mile round.

Ballinrobe in Co. Mayo, in the far west of Ireland, is a market town lying on the River Robe close to Loughs Mask and Carra. There you will find chalybeate springs (renowned for their iron content) and numerous remains of ancient forts, but it is for legendary Irish writer James Joyce that the area is best known.

Ballinrobe racecourse, dating from 1774, is one of Ireland's oldest racecourses. It hosts eight meetings, all in the prime summer months from May to August, including two two-day meetings in May and July. Its final meeting is on a Sunday afternoon, while all the others are in the evening, continuing the Irish-racing tradition of being available to locals as well as holidaymakers. And for those thinking of a post-racing meal, Ballinrobe town, a mile away, boasts a wealth of exceptional places to eat.

My visit in May sees a card of three flat races followed by two hurdles, a chase and a bumper. It is success for the 'small guy' and something of a family affair in the beginners chase when Present Abbey, a five-year-old mare by Presenting, ridden by amateur Robbie Moran, claiming 7 lb, got the better of Ruby Walsh on My Native Donegal. Present Abbey was bred and is owned by Patrick Lambert, and is trained by his cousin Ann Lambert from Killinick, Co. Wexford.

This is the mare's third win in seven runs, and she has also won her only point-to-point. One of her unplaced runs was behind Sidalcea, a half-sister to Best Mate. But she won next time out in a bumper at Limerick ridden by Ann's sister, Clare Lambert.

Her Ballinrobe win is her first run in a chase, having meanwhile won a hurdle at Thurles. It is Ann's first season with a trainer's licence, having previously worked for a number of trainers, and she trains around six plus some point-to-pointers. She rode one point-to-point winner herself, on Joe Long at the Island Hunt meeting. In 2005 Present Abbey went to stud, visiting Old Vic.

Ballinrobe is a typical example of a

Down at the start

small, summer holiday track that has nevertheless seen the debut of a future champion, in this case the lovely Michael Hourigan-trained Dorans Pride.

Ballinrobe makes no pretensions to being one of the 'big boys' and is all the more charming for that. The biggest attendance it has ever seen was nearly 5,000, and that was way back in the early 1990s when Lester Piggott rode there, drawing in the crowds.

For 2005, Ballinrobe has a new weigh-room, and a corporate restaurant with balcony overlooking the attractive course, capable of seating 160 people, who can watch the action from their tables.

One of the more mundane jobs on a racetrack may appear to be that of manning the turnstiles, but it can call for tact and diplomacy. Margaret Byrne is a familiar face issuing the tickets at places as far apart as Wexford and Ballinrobe, Clonmel and Kilbeggan. She sets out from her Tallaght, Dublin, home early in the morning, but says she 'loves the buzz' of racing.

'One time I had Dana [candidate for President of Ireland and one-time Eurovision Song Contest winner] turn up at Ballinrobe with an entourage of six, but no one had told me she was coming – she was canvassing as an MEP at the time – so she had to pay.

'Well, Ballinrobe is only a little meeting, and it already lets in local people wearing the football colours for free. They help swell the crowd after they've been to a match.'

Ballinrobe is an asset to its rural local

'What are your tactics?'

They're off!

Packed stands at a small country meeting on a summer evening – typical of courses such as Ballinrobe

population in ways other than racing, too, for rugby, athletics and cycling events all take place within its grounds.

* * *

On 19 April 1993, the opening meeting of the season, Ballinrobe saw the debut run, and win, of Dorans Pride, who went on to become one of Ireland's best-loved horses for a full decade until his sad death on 13 March 2003.

Back on that spring evening in 1993, Tom Doran's four year old, bred by Hugh Sufferin in Northern Ireland and trained throughout his career by Michael Hourigan in Co. Limerick, was one of eighteen runners for the two-mile River Robe National Hunt flat race. Starting at 7–2 joint favourite with Ozecazey (who finished

ninth), Dorans Pride made light of the soft ground in amateur Brian Moran's hands to beat Ifallelsefails by one and a half lengths; the remaining horses were strung out behind and little was heard of them in the future. But that night there were a few wise heads who guessed they had seen something special in the chestnut gelding by Orchestra out of Marians Pride, and they had.

Dorans Pride was to run in the Cheltenham Gold Cup four times – in which he was third twice, to Mr Mulligan in 1997 and to Cool Dawn the following year; he was to win thirty of his seventy-three races, three on the Flat and twenty-seven over obstacles, and to place twenty-four times; and, incredibly, forty-three of his starts were in Graded races, i.e. the top class.

Ballinrobe and Brian Moran were never reunited with Dorans Pride, though the horse holds a special place in the hearts of both. In his early races, beginning with a win over hurdles in Listowel on only his second racecourse appearance, he was ridden by Kevin O'Brien and Shane Broderick (18 times), and then by Richard Dunwoody (12 times) until his retirement. A.P. McCoy and Paul Carberry put in brief appearances, but the ride was then mainly taken by Paul Hourigan, the professional jockey son of the trainer, who rode him 16 times. Brother Michael junior rode him twice in amateur flat races, while on the Flat Jamie Spencer rode him twice in three days at Royal Ascot in June 2001, and on The Curragh two years earlier.

Dorans Pride brought loyalty from his jockeys, and he rewarded them with consistency on the track. He wasn't out of the first two in his first eight runs until he fell at the second-last in the Royal & SunAlliance Novices Hurdle at the Cheltenham Festival of 1994 in the race won by Danoli. These two favourite horses had several clashes: Dorans Pride was second to him at Fairyhouse in December 1994, but a fortnight later reversed the placings at Leopardstown; in April at Aintree it was the turn of Danoli once more. At the 1995 Cheltenham Festival Dorans Pride became Michael Hourigan's first festival winner when he ran away with the Bonusprint Stayers Hurdle.

Dorans Pride began his chasing career in exactly the same way as he had for bumpers and over hurdles – with a win. It was at his local track of Limerick, and at odds-on in a field of sixteen, that he scored by six lengths. He made it five in a row (seven with his last two hurdle runs), until falling at Thurles in February 1997. His next run was his first Gold Cup when he was third to Mr Mulligan.

The autumn of 1997 saw him score another hat-trick, all in Graded races, including the Kerry National in Listowel, and so the pattern continued. He was at times beaten by horses such as Imperial Call, the 1996 Cheltenham Gold Cup winner, and by the indefatigable Florida Pearl, but he also beat Imperial Call twice (in Clonmel and, in his early days, in a hurdle) and

In running, park-like setting

subsequent Gold Cup winner See More Business before that horse was sold to England. Later in his career he was beaten in a flat race and in a hurdle by Limestone Lad, the phenomenal front-running winner of more than 30 hurdles who successfully reverted to the smaller obstacles when his chasing career failed to materialise; he won four of the five chases he contested, but showed neither the confidence nor fluency that were his hurdling trademarks.

In November 2000, Dorans Pride took part in a handicap flat race at Leopardstown. There were 18 runners and his starting price was 10–1, but no one had told Dorans Pride that he was meant to be past it and he scored by a length. Afterwards Michael Hourigan told the assembled press, 'What can I say about this horse that I haven't said already? He's eleven years old and he's as good as he was five years ago. But for nearly dying of colic a while back, I'm convinced he would have won even more races.'

The finish

But, in fact, the clock was beginning to slow down. Two weeks later, in what was to turn out to be his last win, Dorans Pride lined up for the Morris Oil Chase in Clonmel. With Paul Hourigan in the saddle, he beat Clash of the Gales by two and a half lengths in testing ground. He was to run fifteen more times and to place in nine of them, consistent as ever, but his speed was getting blunted.

Even so, the following summer saw a jaunt to Royal Ascot, where he finished unplaced in the Ascot Stakes and, two days later, third in the Queen Alexandra Stakes.

After running his usual game race in the *At The Races* (formerly Whitbread and now the Betfred) Gold Cup at Sandown in April 2002, he was officially retired. But he hated it. The freedom of grass fields was not for him. This is the case with quite a few thoroughbred racehorses. Some will adapt,

relax, put on weight, stand beneath a spreading chestnut tree contentedly swishing away the flies; others will be tormented by those very insects, miss the mollycoddling of stable life (racehorses in training are among the best cared for animals in the world), lose weight, and pine for work.

Dorans Pride was one such.

The decision was made to return him to training and, all being well, run him in a few hunter chases, the NH races that serve as stepping stones for promising point-to-pointers or as a retirement home for old chasers. He finished second at Leopardstown, and clearly loved being back in the fray, so he was taken to the 2003 Cheltenham Festival for the Foxhunters, a race won by Kingscliff. Sadly at only the second fence, he fell, broke a leg and had to be put down.

Michael Hourigan takes up the story: 'Dorans Pride chose the scene himself. He hated being retired and would have wasted away. He died doing what he did best . . . But it was a big cross to carry. I had three runners that day and all three fell: Beef Or Salmon in the Gold Cup, Hi Cloy and Dorans Pride. With Dorans Pride I felt so sorry for my wife, Anne, and for my daughter, Kay, who looked after him.'

Afterwards, Michael received a number of poison letters from members of the public. 'I burnt them,' he says. Then pauses. 'Wasn't God marvellous in bringing Beef Or Salmon to me? But it is Dorans Pride who put me on the map.'

JUNE

THE CURRAGH

The Curragh (Gaelic for racecourse) is Ireland's sole flat turf course and is home to all five Classics, the premier of which is the Irish Derby, founded in 1866. Although there has been racing here since the 1740s, it is probable that this lovely expanse of land was the venue for chariot racing back in third century AD. It is also said to have been a meeting place of Celtic kings and chieftains. The Curragh is Ireland's answer to Newmarket with its open, gorse-dotted heath and springy, well-drained soil making it perfect to gallop on. Generations of family legends have ridden and trained here: Weld, Prendergast, Oxx, Brabazon, Moore, Harty and Burns, to name but some. The Curragh is also the venue for the Irish Turf Club, founded in 1790, and its administrative headquarters are not far away in Kill.

The flat season kicks off close to 21 March with the first of 20 meetings that end with the close of the flat season in late October. The Irish 1,000 and 2,000 Guineas are held in the third weekend of May; the Irish Derby is near the end of June, the climax of a three-day meeting; the Irish Oaks is held in mid-July; and the Irish St Leger, that somehow keeps producing legendary racehorses – Vinnie Roe made it four in a row in 2004 – takes place in mid-September.

It is a glorious summer day in June 2003 with an immediate air of anticip-

Some of the famous colours worn at Ireland's Turf
headquarters on display at The Curragh

ation. The course is immaculately prepared, looking like a giant lawn with its wide sweeps of mown and rolled grass. In the distance, parallel with the back

Everyone wants to see the winner

straight, cars buzz along the road that bisects The Curragh, their occupants probably unaware of the great day unfolding here. Beyond, the Wicklow Mountains (known colloquially as the Dublin Hills) make a perfect backdrop to the Budweiser Irish Derby stage.

At the entrance is the usual band of lady fruit sellers – they attend many Irish meetings, cajoling racegoers to buy chocolate and fruit. Inside, there are many elegant outfits; the champagne bar is busy. There is only a narrow channel between it and the paddock, making a bottleneck for all those trying to get to the stands – there is a record crowd of 31,136.

I am with friends who have a runner in the second that has already placed in a Listed race and been a good maiden winner. Today he is tackling a Group 2 race and if he does well in this, then next

Good viewing for this pair
at the Irish Derby

Packed stands at the Irish Derby

year's Classics may be on the cards; we share a bottle of bubbly beforehand in case there is no cause to later; sadly that turns out to be the case, for the horse fades out of contention.

But now all attention is focused on the Derby preliminaries. The odds-on favourite is the unbeaten French-trained Dalakhani, winner of the French Derby. Watching them go to the paddock, I like the look of Roosevelt; as they canter to the start, the action of the second favourite, Alamshar, looks outstanding.

It is a magnificent horse race and a privilege to witness. Aidan O'Brien's two pacemakers, Handel and High Country, set a cracking gallop, but on the home turn it is Alamshar and Dalakhani who draw away from the pack, both owned by His Highness the Aga Khan, Dalakhani ridden by Christophe Soumillon and Alamshar,

trained here on The Curragh by John Oxx, ridden by Johnny Murtagh. All the way up the straight they battle it out, two outstanding horses nip and tuck until,

Dalakhani

87

with 50 yards to go, it is the favourite who cracks, and the still-galloping Alamshar wins by half a length. It is the only time in his eight-race career that the French horse is beaten.

Alamshar is by Key of Luck. Key of who? But my astute host has got three mares in foal to him this year . . . In third is Roosevelt, at 150–1! Of the nine runners, six were trained by Aidan O'Brien, yet this outsider is his first home.

By winning this, HH the Aga Khan, who also bred Alamshar, equals the Classic record of his grandfather. The whole aftermath is superbly presented, very slick, with no scrum to the tiny winner's enclosure. Instead, immediately the horses are past the post, a gang carries green-covered tables to the far side of the course by the winning post and a special winner's enclosure is hastily erected. The winner is held back until the other runners have gone, then he is escorted by two army horses, past the stands so that everyone can get a close look, and then back to the presentation area. Even a makeshift weighing room has been erected a few yards away. It is all done with style and panache.

But then that is what one would expect from Ireland's racing headquarters, and one of Europe's best tracks. There are now ambitious plans afoot to ensure The Curragh also boasts the best facilities of any racecourse in Europe.

'The current facilities are not adequate for a premier international venue,' Evan Arkwright, the commercial manager, explains. 'They are old and tired, as was highlighted by the Aga Khan in his speech at the Moyglare Dinner in 2000. It stirred people into action, and the Turf Club set up a grand plan to purchase the Stand Hotel [which is separated from the course by the width of the road]. Negotiations were hush-hush at first but the Aga Khan, who has a big interest here, then generously said he would purchase it and present it to Irish racing.'

This means that the grand plan is on track: the public road is to be re-routed round the back of the hotel and a multi-purpose racecourse facility will be combined with a completely rebuilt hotel.

A plan such as this does not happen like lightning. 'Basically the powers that be are all on-side: the planners, the environmentalists, the road authorities and so on,' says Evan Arkwright. 'We will end up with a facility of huge benefit to the whole area, and to the whole country.' In August 2005, planning permission was granted, with 45 conditions attached to the road plan and 77 to the 72-bed hotel.

The Curragh Plains, to give The Curragh its full title, is a designated national monument, and none of the proposed work will infringe on it. But amenities for the racegoer will be vastly improved, with new lawns, a parade ring, gardens, a retail area, many more seats – and much more comfortable ones – and

an end to the current bottleneck, while aiming to keep a self-contained feel on days less busy than the Classics.

Evan Arkwright points out, 'As the Aga Khan said, whatever we build should still look up to date in 50 years' time.'

* * *

The name Weld has been a leading one through generations of Irish racing and Dermot Weld, the current incumbent of Rosewell House on The Curragh, has become renowned worldwide.

On a visit there, it is easy to see why, for there is an almost tangible atmosphere of contentment about the immaculately run set-up, with horses on lead ropes dotted around the paddock between house and yard, enjoying a pick of the grass not only after work but also before their evening meal.

One name that was not known in racing prior to the mid-1990s was that of Smullen, from the village of Rhode. Rhode? Where? Oh, in Offaly (the back of beyond, in many Irish folk's eyes), the place that used to have a power station (blown up in 2004) and not much more, some would say. But it's a thriving village on a crossroads on a slight (very slight) elevation on the edge of the Bog of Allen. Not horsey country. The schoolkids all play GAA (hurling and Gaelic football), girls as keenly as boys. One of these boys was a bit small and didn't often join in.

Then his older brother started riding for Joanna Morgan, one of the most successful female jockeys turned trainer. Kid brother went along too. Aged 11, Joanna put him on a small pony and taught him to ride, took him hunting with the Tara Harriers. That gave him a horseman's seat and he started riding work on a few of the racehorses.

But then big brother, the one giving him a lift to Joanna's stables, got a job in Canada and stayed there.

So, leaving school at 15, kid brother Pat became apprenticed to Rhode's only trainer, Tom Lacy. He became Champion Apprentice two years running and is remembered with affection by the Lacy family, who gave Pat his first winning ride on board Vicosa at Dundalk, and they also recall his dedication. While the other lads would have soup and rolls at lunchtime, Pat would eat one segment of a tangerine – he did sometimes beg a bar of chocolate off one of Tom and Peg Lacy's children though!

Pat Smullen was on the map. Seems Rhode was too, though it also has links with both a Grand National winner – Sergeant Murphy – and a dual Derby winner – Orby. Sergeant Murphy was reared on a farm at Rathmoyle in Rhode and ran in the National seven times, winning it as a thirteen year old on his fifth attempt in 1923; he was one of those stalwarts who never ran a bad race at Aintree.

Orby was owned by Richard Croker

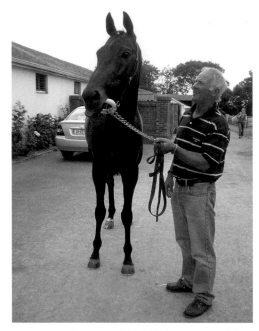

Dermot Weld's head man Tom Gallagher with Vinnie Roe, four-times winner of the Irish St Leger and of the Melbourne Cup

and trained by the forward-thinking Colonel F.F. McCabe whose wife, Mary Sheehy, hailed from Rhode. Orby was, in 1907, the first horse ever to win the Epsom–Irish Derby double, and it was more than half a century before the feat was repeated. Orby's odds for the Irish Derby of 1–10 remain the shortest ever (I believe Arkle was 1–10 for his third Gold Cup, even more unusual in a steeplechase).

Pat Smullen, with a shock of dark brown hair and manly good looks, had that most important quality in a would-be

jockey – the will to win, the competitive spirit (for all he was not sporty), the drive. Ability followed naturally.

And although not from a horsey, let alone racing, background, Pat's was a rural upbringing, surrounded by dogs and farm stock; the sort of upbringing that sees lads and lasses working willingly with racehorses from 7 a.m. until 5 p.m., hardly for the money, wholly for the love of animals. Pat found himself well suited to the world of the thoroughbred racehorse.

And what a world it has shown him.

Racing in America, he won the biggest fillies race, the Matriarch Stakes (Group 1) at Hollywood Park on Dressed to Thrill, as well as the American Derby (Group 2) in Chicago. In Australia he was fourth in the Melbourne Cup on the wonderful Vinnie Roe – the outsider Media Puzzle, his stable companion, won, with Damian Oliver on top. Then a Classic in England: the 2,000 Guineas on Refuse to Bend in 2003 – 'a big hike for my career' – plus the Sun Chariot Stakes, again on Dressed to Thrill – 'one of the best fillies I've ever ridden'. In France the Prix Royal Oak (French St Leger) on Vinnie Roe, to say nothing of an incredible four Irish St Legers on that wonderful horse.

And, of course, Dubai, where he met and later married Ireland's champion amateur rider, now successful trainer, Frances Crowley.

Frances, daughter of trainer Joe, sister-in-law of Aidan O'Brien (married to her

eldest sister Annemarie), grew up longing to race. A natural lightweight, she rode in her first race at 15 years old. She was the first woman to win the amateur championship outright (both sexes and both codes) and dead-heated for it a second time with Willie Mullins.

She spent six months in Australia and says her proudest achievement was riding two winners there as a professional. In all she rode more than 70 winners before embarking on her training career, which has included horses like the brilliant Sackville (18 wins) and the amazing Moscow Express, who won 26 races. In the first of these, a bumper, Moscow was ridden by Frances; Aidan O'Brien trained him in his hurdling career, but then for Frances he won 16 chases, including the Galway Plate. Frances has also trained a Listed winner, Golden Rule, on the Flat. More recently Nil Desperandum has merited an attempt at the 2005 Aintree Grand National, when he finished sixth.

Her ageless father still trains in Kilkenny even though in the summer of 2004 the 75 year old had his kneecap broken when he was riding out in his string and was kicked by another horse. Not that he let that keep him out of the saddle for too long.

Frances reserves special mention for her mother, Sarah, who raised six daughters, the last two being twins – at one time the eldest of all six was only five years old. 'She was marvellous, and a real hard worker.'

Action across part of the nearly 6,000-acre Curragh Plains

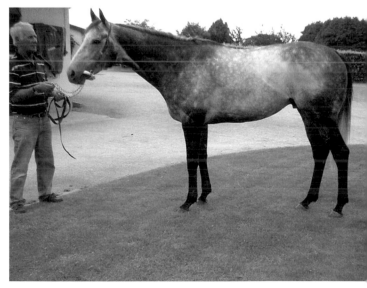

Grey Swallow gave Pat Smullen victory in the 2004 Irish Derby

Champion jockey Pat Smullen, his wife, trainer Frances Crowley, and their daughter, Hannah

It was on her way home from Australia that Frances stopped off in Dubai for a spell, and there met Pat.

Success happened very quickly for Pat Smullen. After his high-flying apprenticeship, he became second jockey to John Oxx, for whom he rode a number of Listed winners. It also saw him on board his first Group 1 winner, Tarascon, in the Moyglare Stakes for the stable of Tommy Stack. That, in only his third season racing and first as a fully fledged rider, gave him his big break. 'Unbelievable,' he recalls.

Less than a year later he was sidelined by a broken collar bone (more often associated with the NH boys), but not until he had won that particular race by

a short head. The horse had then ducked at a shadow and shot Pat to the ground. Ironically the horse, Goldman, was trained by Pat's future wife, Frances.

He was already beginning to take spare rides for John Oxx's Curragh neighbour, Dermot Weld, and when his stable jockey, Mick Kinane, moved on to Aidan O'Brien at Ballydoyle, Pat accepted the job offer from Weld without a moment's hesitation. He was only 20 years old. Two years later, he became Ireland's youngest champion jockey. And still riding work four or five mornings a week.

After their marriage, Pat and Frances tried commuting between her successful training yard in Kilkenny and his base in The Curragh, but now they are the inmates of Clifton Lodge near The Curragh Camp, where the number of horses has doubled and the stable star is the exciting class chaser Nil Desperandum. In the Irish 1,000 Guineas in May 2005 Frances became the first woman in Ireland to train a Classic winner with Saoire. But even these stable stars have to vie for attention with the couple's young daughter, Hannah.

Pat Smullen is the first to admit he's been a beneficiary of 'being in the right place at the right time'. But the success that followed could not have been done without his own dedication, temperament and, ultimately, ability. He would like to add a Breeders Cup race – the Olympic Games of racing – to his CV and, of course, an Epsom Derby.

But at his home track, The Curragh, he achieved his biggest ambition in the summer of 2004 – winning the Irish Derby on Grey Swallow.

* * *

'No foot, no horse.' There was never a truer saying. No horse owner can do without a blacksmith, and he plays a vital role in racing yards. It can be a risky vocation – kicked by a yearling, bitten by a two year old, back crocked by an old monkey – but nevertheless there are those born to it. One such is Sean Bell, 32 years a Curragh farrier.

Born and reared and lived all his life on The Curragh. Grandfather and uncle both racing blacksmiths in Lambourn on his mother's side. Uncle on his father's side, Kevin Bell, trained the 1969 winner of the Irish Grand National, Sweet Dreams, and Bunclody Tiger, winner of the Galway Plate.

'I nearly became an electrician,' says Sean. 'I was 15 and had filled the forms in, but then our neighbour, Mick Halford [a farrier, and father of the current trainer] said if I was interested, be with him on Monday – if you're not there, I'll know you're not coming.'

Sean was there and stayed with him a number of years after completing his apprenticeship until setting up with his brother, Gerard.

It is a trade that has brought him into contact with some of Ireland's best horses – and also brought him a trip of a lifetime to Australia. That was in 1996 when trainer Kevin Prendergast ran Oscar Schindler in the Melbourne Cup. Sean Bell and vet Johnnie Stafford joined head lad Joe Mulholland and stable lad Johnny Sullivan for three weeks, staying in a motel.

'It was the greatest experience of my life,' Sean says. 'Seeing everything: different racing, friendly natives and plenty of craic. The ground came up like a road, which didn't suit our boy; it had been soft for the previous two runnings.'

The only other travelling in Sean's life comes every March when he goes to Cheltenham for his annual week's holiday. It's serious stuff, where drinking is kept to a minimum to keep a clear head for the betting.

'It's my holiday, Sunday to Sunday, then I have to be back for the start of the flat season. It's the only time I ever gamble, so I don't drink.'

Normally he places at least a small bet on any horse at Cheltenham that he has shod. In 2004, when his brother Gerard was ill, he had shod Hardy Eustace for him, but when that horse won the Champion Hurdle at 33–1, Sean 'had completely forgotten' to back him.

He did, however, have £2 on Foinavon, one of four Grand National winners his late uncle, John French, shod, when that horse won the 1967 Grand National at

No foot, no horse: Sean Bell, lifelong Curragh blacksmith

100–1. The other three National winners were Team Spirit, Jay Trump and Anglo.

Sean Bell has shod ten Royal Ascot winners and a dual Classic winner in Blue Wind, who won the Epsom Oaks in 1981, ridden by Lester Piggott, giving Dermot Weld his first Classic winner, and then the Irish Oaks with stable jockey Wally Swinburn in the saddle. Sean also saw to the feet of Katday, dam of Best Mate, prior to her sale a year after Best Mate's birth.

Sean is a bubbly, cheerful chap, living up to the philosophy of laugh rather than cry, and he has never lost a day's work. It's

been close once or twice, as when a horse kicked him and cracked some ribs, but worse was when a horse knocked Sean's paring knife into his hand. 'I was catching a plane that night to go to a family wedding in Lambourn and didn't have time to go to hospital, so the hand was stitched without anaesthetic; that was worse than the cut itself!'

The job can occasionally interfere with his social life, like the time he was due at a party one Sunday lunchtime. A call came that one of 'his' horses had panicked in its box at Leopardstown and torn off two shoes. So off he went to remedy the problem, and the colt ran in its race but got boxed in, putting paid to its chances.

Occasionally Sean will buy a young horse with a view to selling it on in a year or two. He tells the story of how he was offered Mr Mulligan for £800 by the late Jim Rowley. 'He was a two year old with a ewe neck, a big head, and flaxen mane and tail. I told Jim he was the ugliest horse I'd ever seen, I didn't even like to look at him. The day he won the Cheltenham Gold Cup, five years later in 1997, I told myself "You're some judge!"'

Luckily humour is never too far away in Sean's life – and he is a sought-after blacksmith on The Curragh, too.

BELLEWSTOWN

Everything about Bellewstown is summer holiday. Even the funfair keeps revolving while the horses gallop past. It holds its three-day festival every summer, in late June/early July, and until 2005 this was its only meeting.

Now, to the delight of manager Kevin Coleman, another two-day meeting has been added in August, a reward for hard work from Kevin and his team. It will still be very summery, with crowds in shirtsleeves eating candyfloss, going for a ride on the big dipper, enjoying a beer or placing a bet. There is even a public house beside the course, run by my host, Paddy Cummins, himself a keen racegoer.

Deep in Co. Meath, about 23 miles north of Dublin, visitors wind their way round a maze of lanes and come out at Bellewstown racecourse resting on top of the Hill of Crockafotha. On a clear day the Mountains of Mourne can be seen to the north and the River Boyne flows towards the sea to the east. Several quarries can be seen, too; evidence of the growth in road and house building in Ireland.

The centre of the course is a common, dotted with much furze, and there is also a pitch-and-putt course. The furze comes in handy as padding for the hurdles. It is unusual that there are no steeplechase races – these ceased in 1975 because it was proving too difficult to maintain the fences throughout the year for just one meeting.

'But it's possible we may restart them,' Kevin Coleman says, 'because with today's portable fences it would be much easier.'

Plans for the 2005 season, unveiled early in the year, included a ladies' bumper and a new race for the Mullacurry Cup. This is an old point-to-point trophy that has been donated to Bellewstown and was presented at the new meeting in August for a feature three-mile hurdle.

* * *

On the day of my visit, there were three hurdle races, four flat races and a bumper. One of the big differences between English and Irish racing is the daily mixing of flat and NH, which means the flat and jumping jockeys have only about

Funfair and horses in action together at Bellewstown

95

half a card each; and there are usually between one and three days a week without any racing at all. In England there is racing every day, and usually the whole card will be either flat or jumping, so a jockey of either code can have a full book. This is one reason why so many good Irish jockeys move to England to ply their trade.

But Irish racing has so much atmosphere, and visitors like the mixed cards; it suits the smaller country well. Paul Carberry is a fine example of a top jockey choosing to stay in his home country. It means he can continue to go hunting. This is part and parcel of his life. Another who commutes to England, rather than live there permanently, is Ruby Walsh. By riding in both countries, it means he is unlikely to be champion of either, but does that matter? The owners and trainers who put him up know that he is a champion rider, with or without a title. Again, it is quality of life (and in 2005 he won the Irish NH title anyway).

On the other hand, Jamie Spencer, who surprisingly quit the top Irish flat job with Aidan O'Brien in early 2005, was quoted as saying that he missed not being able to race-ride every day. That was his feeling, in spite of having duly become champion flat jockey in his only season in Ireland. This vacancy led to the repatriation of Keiren Fallon, several times British champion when retained by Sir Michael Stoute in Newmarket.

But back to Bellewstown. A 'little' course it might be, but like so many of the other summer tracks, there is evidence everywhere of the management's efforts to cater to their particular crowd, including in this case installing a big screen, used for the first time in 2004. The bends have been banked by the five-furlong chute, another safety asset on a course that is only nine furlongs round.

Racing at Bellewstown goes back to at least 1726, making it possibly the oldest racing venue in Southern Ireland (Down Royal and Downpatrick share a start date of 1685 in the North). In 1780 King George III sponsored His Majesty's Plate, valued at £100. This race was run for 200 years until discontinued by the current Queen in 1980, when the last winner was Weavers Pin, owned and trained by Seamus McGrath, who died in 2005.

On my visit, horse number five, Quintet, should have been a clue for those who back for either sentimental or superstitious reasons. He won the first maiden hurdle race in the masterful hands of Paul Carberry. The next, a one-mile handicap on the Flat, went to number five again, Benwilt Gold, under Pat Cosgrave for trainer Ger Lyons. And in the fifth race it was number five again, a family horse called Ursumman, bred by P.J. Madden, owned by Mrs P. Madden, trained by Niall 'Boots' Madden and ridden by his son 'Slippers'.

I don't think there were five number

fives to win, but the next hurdle race was another family success – a maiden over three miles. This produced victory for the Faheys from Nurney, beside the Irish National Stud in Kildare. P.G. Fahey holds a restricted licence, meaning he is limited to training no more than four horses. This has taken over from the permit, with which the holder could train only family-owned horses, a rule that was sometimes abused. On board the winner, Saor Go Deo, is Peter Fahey (unrelated) for owner Mrs Siobhan Fahey.

Some great NH horses have won at Bellewstown, including triple Champion Hurdler Hatton's Grace among the hurdlers. He won a bumper here in 1946 (bumpers in Ireland are decades older than in England) ridden by his part-owner Dan Corry, better known as a showjumper, before his Cheltenham Triple Crown from 1949 to 1951 ridden by Audrey Brabazon (twice) and Tim Molony. Hatton's Grace was bred by George Harris from Ballykisteen and sold as a yearling for 18 guineas. Apart from his Champion Hurdle treble he also had the speed to win two Irish Lincolns on the Flat and an Irish Cesarewitch. Owned by Mrs Myra Keogh, he was mostly ridden by Aubrey Brabazon, though later by Tim Molony, and trained by the incomparable Vincent O'Brien.

With chasers at Bellewstown including Thomond II, Bright Cherry, Arkloin and Andy Pandy, there is surely a strong case

Crowds enjoy the action at Bellewstown

for bringing back steeplechasing to the Co. Meath venue. Thomond II was to Golden Miller in the 1930s what Mill House was to Arkle in the 1960s: steeplechasers who, without one exceptional, once-in-a-generation rival, would otherwise have been considered the top of their era. Thomond II won the three-mile Duleek Chase at Bellewstown in 1931.

Arkloin, trained by Tom Dreaper, won the Wintergrass Chase at Bellewstown in 1965 and 1966, the same two seasons he won the Totalisator Champion Novice Chase and the National Hunt Chase at the Cheltenham Festival respectively.

Many will remember Andy Pandy flying along in the lead in the 1977 Aintree Grand National, relishing every moment of it, only to fall with John Burke at Bechers Brook second time, while Red Rum went on to record his historic third win in the race.

Bright Cherry will forever be remembered as the dam of Arkle, but it should not be forgotten that she was a good race mare herself. Bellewstown was her local track, only ten miles from her home at Malahow, near Naul in north Co. Dublin. She won the Drogheda Tradesmans Chase here in 1950, a season in which she won three chases.

In 1951 Bright Cherry, a chestnut mare by Knight of the Garter out of Greenogue Princess, retired to stud. Her owners, the Bakers, used inexpensive local stallions, and Bright Cherry produced two filly foals from three matings to Mustang, whose stud fee was under £50. She was then covered by Archive, a failure on the racecourse but beautifully bred by Nearco. This covering produced in 1957 the bay colt that was destined to become the wonder horse Arkle. At the time of his birth, it is said, he looked little other than an ugly duckling.

It will be at least five years before a NH horse begins to prove himself, by which time the stallion may be dead, or the breeders may not have used him again. This was the case with Bright Cherry, though she failed to conceive in the next six years anyway and remained an infrequent breeder. She ran free in a field with a stallion called Ballysway and

produced a winner in Saval Beg. In 1964 – the year of Arkle's first Cheltenham Gold Cup – she gave birth to Golden Sparkle, and in 1966 to Cherry Wine, the year in which Arkle won his third Gold Cup; both these foals were sired by Escart II.

These progenies won, but an attempt to produce to Off Key, a stallion by Nearco, for what would have been an even closer blood relative to Arkle, twice failed.

It was Arkle's good fortune that he was trained throughout his life by the master of Greenogue, Tom Dreaper, and that he had a caring, indeed loving, owner in Anne, Duchess of Westminster. By chance, the connection with Tom Dreaper went back further, for Tom Dreaper had won a point-to-point on Greenogue Princess, the dam of Bright Cherry, and Arkle's grand-dam.

Greenogue Princess, who bred 11 winners for Mrs N.J. Kelly, a member of the Baker family, was by My Prince, who sired Grand National winners Reynoldstown (twice), Royal Mail, Gregalach and Easter Hero, as well as Gold Cup hero Prince Regent.

The dam of Greenogue Princess was Cherry Branch II, who was bought by Nicholas Kelly of Greenogue to hunt with the Ward Union Staghounds. She was also a regular performer at nearby Fairyhouse and won the coveted Ward Hunt Cup three times.

Today Ted Kelly, a cousin of Nicholas Kelly, is well regarded as a steward at

Senior Irish NH handicapper
Noel O'Brien

Fairyhouse. He was a leading amateur rider, which included a win on Roddy Owen on the Flat at Phoenix Park and early rides on Quita Que. This horse went on to be second twice in the Champion Hurdle and was the inaugural winner of the Two Mile Champion Chase at Cheltenham, ridden by Bunny Cox for trainer Dan Moore. Ted Kelly then became a stewards' secretary, firstly in charge of the 'dope patrol' in 1960 and then of discipline in 1972, until he became a NH handicapper in 1985, a role now filled by Noel O'Brien.

When Cherry Branch retired, she bred twelve winners, including Cherry Tree (who won two flat races, six hurdles and three chases), Prince Cherry and Greenogue Princess.

So it can be seen that although Arkle's sire, Archive, was on the 'take-a-chance' side, there were plenty of winners on the dam's side. Bright Cherry was one of four full sisters, all by Knight of the Garter.

Bright Cherry was foaled in 1944, and her first run was at Baldoyle on 31 July 1948, a now defunct track on the east coast near Dublin airport between Malahide and Howth. Ridden by Tom Dreaper's stable jockey at that time, Eddie Newman, she finished third of six in a two-mile hurdle. She was quite small but speedy and a good jumper, and on good-to-firm ground she could stay two and a half miles. Bright Cherry ended her racing career at the top of the handicap, having won one hurdle and six chases and placed eleven times; her wins included the Easter Handicap at Fairyhouse and, of course, the Drogheda Tradesmans Chase at Bellewstown. But it is as the dam of Arkle that she is immortalised.

Three Aintree Grand National winners kick-started their careers at Bellewstown on top of the Hill of Crockafotha: the aptly named Drogheda (1898), Shaun Spadah (1921) and Freebooter (1950).

Drogheda, as his name implies, was bred in Co. Louth. Its county town of that name is only six miles from Bellewstown. Drogheda's debut in 1894 was on his local course in a race for two year olds over five furlongs; he returned in 1897 and won a chase, the year he also won the Galway

Plate. The following year saw his only attempt at the Grand National, when the going was described as 'very heavy and bad', and the weather as a 'blinding snowstorm'.

There were twenty-four runners of whom ten finished – not bad in the conditions, but it was Drogheda who coped with them best, beating Cathal. Down the field in seventh was Grudon, who, three years later, was to run in another 'blinding snowstorm' and on ground that was 'very deep, course white with snow'. It is said that a coat of butter on the soles of his feet prevented the snow from balling.

Drogheda was only six years old when he won the Grand National, and it was a year that Manifesto was not in the line-up: during the period from 1895 to 1904 Manifesto ran in the race eight times, more than any other horse in Aintree's long history. Bred in Co. Meath by Harry Dyas, Manifesto won the Grand National twice and was third three times from the age of seven to sixteen years, carrying up to as much as 12 st. 13 lb. He is my own favourite Grand National horse.

Shaun Spadah was a dual winner of the Drogheda Tradesmans Chase in 1917 and 1918. He won the 1921 Grand National ridden by Fred Rees, one of the finest jockeys of his day. He needed all his skill that day, for on slippery ground he was the only one of thirty-five starters who put in a clear round. Several fell at the first, and only two were left standing at the last where The Bore fell. The Bore, All White and Turkey Buzzard all remounted (Turkey Buzzard four times) to finish. The following year Shaun Spadah fell at the first himself, a fate that has befallen a surprising number of previous winners over the years, not least Aldaniti.

Freebooter, bred in Co. Waterford, survived a monumental blunder at the Chair in the 1950 Grand National; jockey Jimmy Power lost both stirrups and clung precariously to his horse's neck before regaining his seat, going on to win the great race by 15 lengths from fellow Irish runner Wot No Sun. Freebooter had won his bumper at Bellewstown in 1946.

In more recent times Bellewstown flat winners have included the joint champion two year old of 1995, Almaty, who won his maiden here; Sir Azzaro, who became the first American-trained two year old to win in Ireland, at Bellewstown in 2002; and in the same year Liberman won the Eddies Hardware Goodbye to the Hill Bumper, trained by Paddy Mullins, prior to his famous Cheltenham bumper victory of 2003, by which time he had been moved to England.

But in some ways the best remembered Bellewstown winner is a horse called Yellow Sam, who, in 1975, pulled off one of the country's biggest betting coups through the renowned Barney Curley – and in the summer of 2005 this infamous punter agreed to return to the holiday track as a guest, marking the 30th anniversary of the day when he reputedly emptied the bookies' satchels of some £260,000. Back then he'd booked four rooms in a local hotel and, speaking in the summer of 2005, he recounted to two Bellewstown committee members how he sat on a bed counting out the money into sacks.

JULY

KILBEGGAN

Kilbeggan, Co. Westmeath, epitomises the laid-back love of racing among Irish people, and nowhere is local loyalty more apparent than here. These are the summer evenings or weekend afternoons, seven of them between May and September, when the community turns out for its course. A live band plays in the beer tent throughout, the bookmakers do a brisk trade, and the Tote is well supported.

The stands are packed, and the little hill that makes a natural grandstand has its spectators too – as well as a few children rolling down its bank every now and again. It's like this even when it's wet; my first visit was on a damp May evening, but what struck me most was the number of people present. When in July of 2003, I paid my first visit to the Midlands National, the place was packed out. Most people were dressed in open-necked shirts and jeans, but there was a splattering of smartly dressed ladies. There were many more men than women in the crowd, as is standard, enjoying a beer, some banter and most of all a bet.

To say there was either a big build-up or a sense of anticipation before the feature race would be an exaggeration. Kilbeggan people are not like that. They enjoy all the races at all the meetings.

A full complement of sixteen parade before the Midlands National, worth €50,000 to the winner; it is a handicap run over two miles seven furlongs. I pick out two possibles on form, but then number one comes into the paddock. He looks all over a steeplechaser and although he is sweating I keep thinking what a swell fellow he looks. His top weight is reduced, I see, by the booking of an amateur who claims 7 lb off his brown back. Other horses are ridden by top jockeys like Norman Williamson, over from England especially to ride the favourite, Royal County Buck, with a weight of only 9 st. 12 lb, for trainer Tony Martin and owners the Dunsany Racing Syndicate. Paul Carberry, Timmy Murphy, David Casey and Barry Geraghty, the man of 2003, all have live hopes.

But I still like number one and, last of the big spenders, put a couple of euro to place on him. He is called Just In Debt (!) and is trained by P.M.J. Doyle in Thurles

Viewing from the hill as the runners pull up for a race on this gently undulating right-handed track

for the Absent Friends Syndicate. He is ridden by Mr Derek O'Connor.

Joining the throng on the bank, we watch an enthralling steeplechase in this pretty Midlands setting. The runners have settled down as they head out on the second circuit. Royal County Buck moves steadily forward and as they come to the last fence, five horses are there with a chance, a handicapper's dream. It is nip and tuck all the way to the line and, in a photo finish, the favourite beats my horse by a short head.

There are happy celebrations among the winner's connections in the ring. Course manager and secretary Paddy Dunican directs the line-up, and a polished MC makes the introductions and says something interesting about the winner, as he does after every race, adding to the moment as the proud owner steps forward to receive the trophy. Later I discover this is Colm Murray of the RTÉ 1 sports desk – no wonder he did the job so well.

Colm Murray grew up in Moate, Co. Westmeath, and Kilbeggan was his local track; from the age of nine or ten he was a regular visitor, accompanied by his father. 'Right from the start, as a young fella, I loved it for its atmosphere,' he remembers. 'There was flat racing then, and I remember a horse winning called Long Long Ago trained by Clem Magnier. I was in the outfield area, where there was a funfair and other attractions, and I watched the racing from the hill; it was a fabulous place for a kid.'

Colm went into broadcasting as an

RTÉ's Colm Murray interviews Michael O'Leary after the Midlands National

'I used to haunt him for his autograph, and one day I asked him to sign beside the name of Duffcarrig, a really good handicapper. He said, "Do you back horses?" and I said only if you are riding, and he advised me not to be a gambler.

'I failed to take notice of that, but I'm hanging on in there. A bet adds to a brilliant day out racing.'

Back in Kilbeggan after the Midlands National, a large bouquet of flowers suddenly appears, then a number of those smartly dressed ladies walk into the paddock and I realise why. There has been a best-dressed lady competition going on, and these are the finalists. Very elegant they are, and I soon discover this is a part of many feature meetings.

Not that smart ladies are anything new to Kilbeggan, for in the mid-1950s a visitor to the races was film actress Rita Hayworth, who turned many heads and stole numerous hearts. That was on 11 May 1953, when Prince Aly Khan won the Westmeath Plate, riding his own filly Ynys.

There have been ups and downs in Kilbeggan's history since it was founded by a group of gentlemen in 1840 for a Challenge Cup worth 40 guineas. Over the next 15 years racing took place at various locations in the neighbourhood, including the present one, but then lapsed for more than 20 years. Its revival in 1879 was due in part to the Locke family, owners of the world's oldest licensed distillery (for Irish

announcer. He worked in the news before moving into sport, 'meaning my hobby became my work', he says. 'I was paid not only to go to Kilbeggan, but also to places like Cheltenham, Auteuil and Longchamp.'

Colm's childhood idol was Pat Taaffe. 'He was an icon throughout Ireland, every quarter of the country, transcending every sport; he was a superstar, a household name as much as Lester Piggott was. He made his name before Arkle, winning the Grand National on Quare Times for Vincent O'Brien, but more than anything he was very warm-hearted and much loved. He had a charisma that endeared him to people.

105

whiskey), whose operation in Kilbeggan is today part of the tourist trail – they provided a field for the races for a number of years until, after another lapse, the races were revived again in 1901 in the present location in Lochnagore and have continued there every year since, except during the Second World War.

There were difficult times in the 1950s and '60s, when the voluntary committee running the meeting had its financial assistance withdrawn. Over the same period the only other Midlands meeting, at Mullingar, was having similar difficulties. Poor Mullingar succumbed, and on the back of its demise Kilbeggan prospered, especially when it changed to be an all-NH meeting in 1971. The hard work of its committee from that time, including the purchase of the land and the opening of its refreshment and admin complex in 1990,

Best-dressed ladies with manager
Paddy Dunican

was rewarded that year when it gained the title of Racecourse of the Year.

Improvements did not stop there, and since then a service road has been provided and the concourse area has been resurfaced. The track has been widened and extended to allow for larger fields, the enclosure enlarged to accommodate its corporate tented village and in 1999 its new £1 million corporate pavilion was opened.

As recently as 1992 there were only three meetings per year; that was doubled to six and is currently on seven (having been eight in 2004). The Midlands National was an inspired addition in 1997, when another film celebrity, director Neil Jordan, was one of the owners of the winner, Cristy's Picnic.

There was a time when a vet by the name of J.J. Parkinson stabled his horse at Dalystown the night before racing. The next day his son, Emmanuel, rode six out of six winners. Another occasion, but not one for joy, was when a loose horse, trained by Ruby Walsh senior and ridden by Ted Walsh, drowned in a pond, his head being caught up in part of the bridle, preventing him from getting free.

But most tragic by far was that sad, sad day in August 2003 when jockey Kieran Kelly was killed. Kieran was a jockey of much more than mere promise.

As one of eight children from a non-horsey family at Derrinturn, Co. Kildare, he and a friend, both aged about eleven, were looking over a gate at some racehorses. Trainer Micky Flynn invited them in and offered them pocket money to do a few jobs. 'Come back tomorrow, if you like,' he said. Only Kieran did.

Micky taught him to ride, sent him to the apprentice school in Kildare, where he won an award, and gave him his first winner, a nine-furlong event at Tipperary on Angel From Heaven, two days after Kieran's 18th birthday. He also provided him with his first jumping win in a hurdle race at Dundalk in 1997. When Micky retired, Kieran moved on to Dessie Hughes, became stable jockey and won the Royal & SunAlliance Novices Hurdle at Cheltenham with Hardy Eustace in 2003. He was also second in the 2001 Irish Grand National on Rathbawn Prince, the year he had his first ride in the Grand National on Dark Stranger for Martin Pipe, and also won three hurdle races in a row on Colonel Braxton.

'It was his gentleness, kindness, care and love that marked Kieran on and off horseback,' Dessie said at his funeral. 'We will miss his good humour and his welcome of "Bonjour" each morning directed at the Frenchman in our yard.'

The 25-year-old Kieran had won a race earlier in the Kilbeggan card – Barrack Buster, for Martin Brassil – before going out on his last fateful ride. Racing the next day in Gowran Park was called off as a mark of respect; all those involved in the sport were stunned, and mourned his tragic death.

Three short months later flat-apprentice Sean Cleary, whose home was in Co. Westmeath, not far from Kilbeggan, died following a fall at Galway. Sean was twenty-two years old and had ridden fourteen winners that season, one of them on a horse that was being filmed for television programme *Only Fools Buy Horses*. Sean had done particularly well to win in a photo finish, and the whole series portrayed the fun of racing. That Sean was not alive to see the end product was devastating. His sense not only of fun but also of responsibility, and especially his likeability, were evident in the programme.

Ireland is a small, close-knit country that still pays special attention to family life, and the sense of grief among the even smaller community of horse racing was almost tangible after these two tragedies. It is extremely rare to have a death, and both were a terrible price to pay in a wonderful sport that has such an enthusiastic following, none more so than at Kilbeggan.

Full flight over a fence in Kilbeggan

KILLARNEY

Killarney is a world-renowned tourist stop, the starting and stopping point of the scenic Ring of Kerry. Surrounded by the majestic Macgillycuddy's Reeks and the sparkling Lakes of Killarney, the town itself is sometimes called 'Heaven's Reflection'.

Killarney is one of those places that you accept is full of tourists and love it just the same for it has an immense charm and is full of genuine character. Brightly painted houses and shops are often adorned with colourful flower baskets. The town teems with pubs and places to stay, and with jolly jaunting cars, the horse-drawn traps that convey visitors around; passengers may see artists, buskers, Kerry dancers, cyclists, and hikers fresh off the hills. You also know that 'off the beaten track' is a mere pebble's throw away, but exploring the vibrant, colourful little town first is a must.

This includes the racecourse, for it is part of the town, the more so since new houses have encroached upon its environs. But then the whole of Ireland has become such a flourishing country that this is a picture repeated at many once rural courses. For Ireland to continue being successful, it must have houses for its populace – its workforce – to live in and let the memories of mass emigration, poverty and famine dim ever further into the past.

Killarney races bring together not only the locals, who come en masse, but many visitors too, from all parts of the island,

from Great Britain and from America. It is not just a 'pretty, pretty' place to visit, for it has a sense of aura about it. Maybe this is because it is so steeped in history: 2,000 years ago the Celtic warriors known as the Fianna used to dwell here and along the banks of the River Flesk, which borders the course and flows into Loch Leane.

There used to be two racecourses in the area between the years of 1827 and 1901. There was then a lapse of 35 years until the current course came into being in 1936. Eleven years later, its famous racing festival was founded. Killarney now hosts three meetings a year, this main one in July, covering four days and featuring a good mix of races, and preceded by a three-day mini-festival in May. A final one-day meeting signs off the summer in September. The course also boasts a nine-hole golf course (one of many in the area) that is open all year.

Killarney has a home-bred general manager in John Looney. His parents' home is 100 yards from the track and as a young teenager he used to earn pocket money on race days by manning the turnstiles or selling racecards. After college in Dublin and working in San Diego for a few years, John jumped at the chance to take on the Killarney job, a case of full circle.

'I'm discovering that beginners chases are expensive to put on, because I have to replace so much birch,' he says.

'The three Kerry courses are very much part of our country make-up; we might be a long way from The Curragh, but we still know how to put on good racing.'

On the day of my visit there is a light rain, and the mist covers the hills. When it clears, those beautiful peaks reveal themselves and a glimpse of the shimmering lake. The racecourse itself is well tended: the paddock is bounded by a neatly trimmed privet hedge growing between white rails and two tall yucca trees grow from a mound in the middle. Everywhere the grass is mown immaculately.

The eight-race card starts off with a hurdle and then a chase, followed by six flat races. The bookmakers tout for trade – there are always a lot of them at Irish race meetings – and one is Ellen Martin. Blonde and smartly dressed in bright-red trousers, shoes and a waterproof hat, she is one of three female bookies here today in the male-dominated business.

'I've been a bookie for ten years . . . there are a few others, mostly wives and daughters, they attract the business. I've got just enough punters here to make a good book and they like to have a flutter with me.'

Of all the winners the most impressive is the Tom Hogan-trained Rooftop Protest. He wins a two-mile one-furlong flat handicap by the proverbial country mile in the hands of Robbie Burke for owner Peter McCutcheon.

Four runners go to post for the

Evening action at Killarney, against a backdrop of the Macgillycuddy's Reeks

View on a damp day

J.M. Allen and Tobar Na Bron: winners at Killarney

Birch flies in the beginners chase

steeplechase, trained by four top Irish trainers – Arthur Moore, Dermot Weld, Eddie O'Grady and Pat Hughes – and ridden by four top Irish jockeys – Conor O'Dwyer, David Casey, Barry Geraghty and Jim Culloty. In the end it is the David Casey-ridden Mutakarrim, trained by Dermot Weld and fresh off the Flat, who carries the day for joint owners Michael Smurfit, Mrs Eliza Berry and Lynch Long.

The jumping over, Jim Culloty repairs to the Jim Culloty Bar, where he shakes countless hands proffered him and answers just as many questions.

'What's going to win the next race?' one fan asks.

'Not a clue, it's flat,' he answers patiently.

We chat, and he says, 'What do you think of this place? It's lovely here, isn't it?' He looks around proudly. It's his home. Killarney's son is back in Killarney, if only briefly.

It is during the summer that he is able to ride quite regularly in his native land, when most of the English jumpers that he will be riding for Henrietta Knight later in the year are turned out for their summer holidays.

He spends as much of his time in Ireland as his English riding commitments permit, either on the Co. Cork farm that he and his wife Susie have bought near Churchtown, or riding at Irish meetings (mainly the festivals, to keep his eye in and his purse from emptying), visiting a local point-to-point, or hunting.

He was out one Monday with the

Lady bookmaker Ellen Martin

Duhallow Foxhounds – not one of their vintage days, as it turned out, but friendly, and a mix of jumping banks and ditches, or drains as they're known in Ireland. On this particular day Jim, hero of the last three Cheltenham Gold Cups with Best Mate, was riding a hireling. But instead of the usual safe-conveyance hunter-type, it was a thoroughbred that promptly crashed into the first two ditches, plastering himself and his hapless jockey in thick mud. By the time he reached the third, Jim wisely dismounted and sent the horse over on his own.

What a relief it was to see Jim win a chase at Wincanton five days later, especially as the horse, Rathbawn Prince, is owned by his pregnant wife. But then even as a lad he had the guts and the skill to make a top jockey. When other boys were off playing football, Jim would be out on a pony, or hanging around the local stables. There were no horses in his family background, though his father, Donal, always enjoyed a regular punt in the local betting office, and once had a horse in training near Gowran. That's where Jim used to work as a lad in his summer holidays, and when racehorses became a passion that he never lost.

* * *

Jim Culloty at home in Killarney, chatting to fans inside 'his' bar

The people of Kerry are understandably proud of their jockey son. He would think nothing of riding a little-schooled horse in a point-to-point for someone and presenting it perfectly at all the fences in a manner that reminds some spectators of Adrian Maguire or the late Pat Taaffe.

When he won the Amateur Riders Championship in England in 1995–96, his first season with Henrietta Knight, the town of Killarney put on a civic reception for him. So imagine what it was like in 2002 when he won both the Cheltenham Gold Cup (Best Mate) and the Grand National (Bindaree) within a month of each other. Jim said that at least 200 people he'd never met shook his hand and congratulated him.

The feat helped put Killarney on the map, says retired racecourse manager Mr Michael Doyle, and the racecourse promptly named its main bar after him. 'We have plenty of good young lads and Jim proved you can go to the top even if you come from Killarney.'

He adds that Kerry boasts three racecourses – Tralee, Listowel and Killarney – but 'it takes an entity like Jim' to help publicise that fact.

The year after winning the Grand National, Jim won the Irish version on Timbera at Fairyhouse. He then momentously went on to win the next two Cheltenham Gold Cups with Best Mate.

Success has not in anyway spoiled Jim Culloty; he is a fine ambassador for racing, and an excellent son of the Kingdom of Kerry and his home town of Killarney. In July 2005, Jim annouced his retirement from the saddle; he now plans to train from his Co. Cork farm.

GALWAY

If you ever go across the sea to Ireland,
Then maybe at the closing of your day;
You will sit and watch the moon rise over
   Claddagh,
And see the sun go down on Galway Bay.

Wherever in the world there are Irish men and women, so *Galway Bay* is sure to be sung. Every July there will be thousands of the Irish in Galway with many a singsong after the races each night, all seven days that make up the Galway Festival.

Two hundred thousand beat their way through the gates of Ballybrit, four miles north of the city centre, for the races, and the whole of Galway city and county becomes immersed in 'the Week'. Most race days have a different theme for the public: Monday is the Big Bash; Thursday is Ladies Day complete with best-dressed-person competition, giving the gentlemen a chance of a prize; Sunday is Mad Hatters Day, when visitors are invited to 'wear a mad hat to bring a smile to Galway faces'.

But *the* day is Wednesday, the day of the Galway Plate.

When I first visited Galway, I thought a plate at a summer meeting would be a flat race, but all Ireland knows, of course, that this is one of the country's most prestigious handicap steeplechases. Founded in 1869, the two-mile six-furlong race has seen some epic battles over the nearly rectangular course.

There has been organised racing in the area since the mid-thirteenth century when match races on the Flat were run under the auspices of the King's Plate Articles. There is also a record of a five-day meeting in 1764 at Knockbarron, near Loughrea, but the first steeplechases were held at Kiltulla, a little east of Galway near Oranmore, until in 1868 flooding meant the races were moved to their present location at Ballybrit and with them, the founding of the Galway Plate.

From the start, the new venue, lent free of charge by Capt. Wilson Lynch, was popular, some 40,000 people turning up for the first day: Tuesday, 17 August 1869. The entrepreneur behind it all was one Lord St Lawrence, MP for Galway, who had been influential in the founding of Punchestown. With the assistance of his co-stewards – Lord Clanricard, Lord Clarmorris, Capt. Blake Forster, Henry S. Persse, Pierce Joyce, George Morris and Valentine Black, like him, keen hunting and steeplechasing men – his efforts resulted in scenes reminiscent of the first Grand National at Aintree 30 years earlier. Publicity was likewise good and so many people turned up for the two-day meeting that some had to be accommodated via makeshift arrangements, be it two (or even four) in a bed, or camping in Eyre Square, Galway. Street vendors and pickpockets arrived on the scene probably in about equal numbers. There were four races on both days, the main attraction being the Galway Plate for a hundred sovereigns, an open handicap steeplechase of two and a half miles. Among the eight fences to be negotiated were two stone walls. Tenant farmers were allowed to ride in the Glenard Plate for £50, and there was also a Visitors Plate for amateur gentlemen riders. The local railway company agreed to transport horses there for free provided they had previously run in a race, and this concession helped encourage entrants. It wasn't only the horses that travelled by train, for special passenger trains were put on from all over the country for Galway. The result was an unqualified success, and so the future of Galway races was predicted as being 'superior to any other provincial races in the country'.

Then, as now, the races were deemed a social success, and the following year saw a number of improvements designed not only for better racing, but also for an even bigger public following. The organisers copied Punchestown in building a rattling double bank and adding extra fly fences. Liberator and Drogheda, two future Aintree Grand National winners, were early victors.

The Beasley brothers rode a good few winners from the 1870s to the 1890s; in 1910 the winner, Ashbrooke, was ridden by Mr Harry Ussher. Not only did the Ussher family support the meeting from the outset right up until Harry's death in 1957, but they also trained a total of seven Galway Plate winners, and in 1920 Harry trained the winners of all the races on the opening day, except for the plate itself.

Aubrey Brabazon scored three times as a rider, twice on Swindon Glory, one of few dual winners, although Tipperary Boy won the Plate three times at the turn of the nineteenth into the twentieth century, the only horse to have achieved this feat. Other dual winners have been Clonsheeva in the 1920s, Amber Point in the 1950s, Ross Sea and Royal Day in the '60s and Life of a Lord in 1995–96 for trainer Aidan O'Brien, and Ansar, 2004–05.

Ross Sea, ridden by Stan Mellor, who came over from England, was one of four consecutive winners trained by Phonsie O'Brien, the other two being Carraroe and Blunt's Cross, but even more successful as a trainer of the plate was Paddy Sleator, who trained seven winners between 1948 and 1969. He was also particularly successful at Punchestown and Killarney, where he once won eight races with six horses over the three days.

Bobby Beasley, grandson of Harry, won two Cheltenham Gold Cups (on Roddy Owen in 1959 and Captain Christy in 1974), a Champion Hurdle, a Grand National – and four Galway Plates. The first of these was on Knight Errant in 1957 for Paddy Sleator, and again for him on Sparkling Flame in 1960. He rode the following year's winner, Mr F.L. Vickerman's Clipador, and in 1963 Bobby was on board the winner again, this time Lord Fermoy's Blunt's Cross, trained by Phonsie O'Brien.

Right from its enterprising start, Galway has always been innovative and quick to catch the race-going public's eye. The broadcasting of races from Galway and The Curragh began in 1929, and Galway was first televised in 1963, four years after the first sponsors arrived when the meeting was extended to three days. A new stand was built in 1971 along with an administration block. In 1979 the Galway Plate was sponsored for the first time, and the winner of the Hygeia Ltd Galway Plate that year was the Edward O'Grady-trained Hindhope. He had trained the previous year's winner, too: J.P. McManus's Shining Flame. The first five-day meeting took place in 1974 and when it was extended to six days in 1982, it became the longest Irish meeting. It capped itself in 1999 by becoming a seven-day meeting, and still it thrives. I have even heard rumours that it might yet become an eight-day festival. A €1.4 million weighing room, media centre and administration block was opened in 2004. Among a lot else the new facilities included a sauna for female jockeys.

* * *

There were landmarks for the fairer sex in 1987 and 1989 when Anne Collen first trained Randross to win for her father, Standish Collen, and two years later her sister Sarah rode the winner, Bold Flyer (trained by Jim Dreaper), again for their father.

Randross had won four chases under the guidance of Jim Dreaper, but after the

Packed stands every day at the Galway Festival. A new stand will be ready in 2007

death of her mother in 1985, Anne Collen took out a permit and trained the horse from home. A year later he won a chase at Leopardstown for her, piloted by Martin Lynch, encouraging her to enter him for the Galway Plate in the summer of 1987. There, ridden by Ken Morgan in a field of 22, he entered the record books as the first female-trained winner of the plate.

Bold Flyer was only six years old when he took part and there were those who felt he should not be running in the plate at all, let alone with a lady amateur rider on board. Sarah's credentials were good – she had become the first lady rider to win the historic Conyngham Cup at Punchestown two years earlier, riding Feltrim Hill Lad, and her initial third on Bold Flyer had been followed

Happy connections, filmed by RTÉ after the Galway Plate

Martin also enjoy hunting with the Wards.

So Sarah Collen took her place in the plate on level terms with the professional jockeys; she led from flag-fall and romped home in a record time that still stands today. Currently both sisters remain the only winning female trainer and rider of the prestigious plate. Sarah, slim and vivacious, was equally competent riding on the Flat and was champion lady amateur rider in 1985. She still hunts, prepares yearlings for the sales with her husband, Ray Jennings, from their home near Naas, and competes in local shows. She also watches her daughters, Claire and Phoebe, ride with success.

On hearing that Galway has installed a sauna for lady riders, Sarah laughed. 'That's enough to make me want to stage a comeback!'

by two all-the-way successes at Gowran Park and Roscommon. Not for nothing was Sarah the daughter of her father.

She and Anne had grown up in Co. Meath hunting with the Ward Union, which has a worldwide reputation for being fast and furious, where no quarter is given and none expected, where the ditches are huge and the falls numerous, and where father Standish, who died in 2004, was a renowned horseman, successful point-to-point rider and member of the Turf Club. Among the jockeys past and present that currently hunt with the Wards are Nina and Paul Carberry; Ross, Norman, Barry, Jill and Holly Geraghty and their father Tucker; Gordon and Joe Elliott; Robert Power and leading lady point-to-point rider Claire McMahon. Trainers Tom Taaffe and Tony

Galway Plate-winner Ansar, David Casey up, trained by Dermot Weld for Mrs K. Devlin

Rory Cleary, runner-up in the apprentice's championship

To say Galway is popular is putting it mildly; trying to get around on Galway Plate day makes Gold Cup day at Cheltenham seem a doddle. The jockeys' caps may be all that is seen of a race unless a place has been found in a stand. But no one seems to mind, as they pack six deep around the parade ring, or cram into the new millennium stand, or push their way towards a bookie's board. It is no surprise that when it comes to betting, Galway beats all comers. Some €3.32 million was bet with the bookmakers on Galway Hurdle day (Thursday) alone in 2004; in 2005 the figure was €4,292,715 and the attendance was 46,498, a national record. The cumulative amount bet during the whole week in 2004 on the Tote and with bookmakers amounted to €24 million, a figure that in 2005 was a staggering €26,882,034, when it was announced that a new €20 million stand will be built by

2007. The Galway Hurdle is the richest hurdle in Ireland and what a race it produced in 2004.

Sometimes a trainer makes a mark on a particular race, just as a horse may. In the Galway Hurdle it is a young trainer and former Wexford hurler who has made it his stamping ground in recent years. Paul Nolan won it with Say Again in 2002 and was beaten by three-quarters of a length the following year with Cloone River. He then did something that several Irish trainers attempt – planning ahead to the next year. Determined to go one better in '04, he preserved the hurdle rating of the Un Desperado gelding by running him only on the Flat. Cloone River was no slowcoach in that sphere either, winning two good handicaps, but it was the Galway Hurdle

Cathy Gannon, Champion Apprentice

that Cloone River was 'laid out for'. Ante-post odds of 12–1 became 5–1 on the day, only to tumble to 7–2 at the off. And it was as if there weren't twenty-two other talented opponents, the next shortest price being 12–1, covering six horses.

Come the moment, come the man. In spite of being nearly brought down in running, Cloone River, cleverly ridden by John Cullen and carrying 10 st. 7 lb, ran out a two-length winner from Gemini Guest, 9 st. 13 lb, and Mirpour, 10 st. 2 lb. There were many happy – and considerably wealthier – connections celebrating afterwards.

Paul Nolan freely admitted to the press, 'We decided not to run him over hurdles again so as to protect his [handicap] mark. We could have run him in good conditions hurdles, but his rating would have gone up and he wouldn't have won today.'

Simple, really.

The Galway Hurdle had played a part in the previous day's 2004 Galway Plate, for the winner, Ansar, had won the hurdle in 2001. And, like Cloone River, he hadn't run in a jumping race for a year before winning this event, 'warming up' with a couple of flat runs instead. It was the third plate winner for Dermot Weld, and he became the first trainer since Paddy Sleator (Knight Errant) in the 1950s to win both feature events with the same horse. Ansar is a marvellous little horse who, with this victory, made it seven wins at Galway from nine runs on the course, making him a real course specialist.

In 2005 this well-bred son of Kahyasi had to carry top weight of 12 st., reduced by 3 lb due to the presence of claiming rider Denis O'Regan, 'lent' by Noel Meade, on his back. Denis gave him a copy-book ride and, always in touch, fencing superbly and hugging the inside rail, Ansar drew seven lengths clear on the run-in for a supremely popular victory, during a week which also saw trainer Dermot Weld gain his 3,000th domestic winner.

The most poignant moment in the whole week at Galway 2004, however, was the win on Tuesday of apprentice Rory Cleary in the one-mile one-hundred-yards McDonogh EBF Handicap, because his talented elder brother, Sean, had died following a fall on the same course the previous October. Ironically, Rory's win was on Palace Star, who had won the race in which Sean had suffered his fatal fall.

There was a hug for Rory in the winner's enclosure from his mother, Kathleen, and, naturally, many free-flowing tears. Rory ended the season runner-up to Cathy Gannon in the Apprentices Championship. Life goes on.

One of the most memorable events ever to take place at the racecourse had nothing to do with horses and all to do with Ireland's mainly devout Roman Catholics. His Holiness the late Pope John Paul II visited the venue in September 1979 when, to a crowd of hundreds of thousands, he held an outdoor Mass in the grounds.

AUGUST

TRAMORE

For Tramore, think vacation. Within yards of the seaside, the tiny course is both attractive and unusual – and there is definitely a holiday atmosphere.

The brown signposts for tourists have so many fingers on them that it can be difficult to spot the one for the racecourse in amongst the B&Bs, golf clubs, beaches and assorted other attractions, but it is still easy to find.

In its early years from 1785, Tramore races were held on the Black Strand and were so popular that by mid-August 1807 it held a six-day meeting. It was all flat to begin with – steeplechases were incorporated at a later stage – but the course was in constant danger from stormy seas, and in 1911 it was irreparably breached. Undaunted, the racecourse company relocated slightly inland to its current venue on Graun Hill.

Tramore racecourse might be small, but it is big in ideas. In 2002, on its traditional New Year's Day meeting, it became the first Irish racecourse to use the euro, and back in 1971 it had been the first to introduce decimalisation. It was the only course in the whole of Europe to race on New Millennium Day, 1 January 2000.

The wisdom of its staging was swiftly proved as more than 10,000 people flocked to the venue, smashing all previous records. It was the same with the betting. To be there that day was truly memorable, as enlightened manager Sue Phelan recalls,

'We had taken a big gamble to stage the meeting when so many other tracks had opted to defer their fixture, but as soon as the tapes went up for the first race and I heard the deafening roar from the stands, I knew we had made the right decision and aptly enough the horse that won the first race of the millennium was called No Problem.' At the end of it all, there was a spectacular fireworks display.

At the helm are a group of 90 local shareholders, including Mean Fiddler concert promoter Vince Power and successful businessman Peter Queally, and it is these innovators who steered the course to victory in the 1998 Irish Racecourse of the Year award – only one year after the new owners took on the refurbishment project. To date, over €5 million has been spent on improving facilities in and around the enclosures and on the track.

The two-mile six-furlong Wilf Dooley Chase, Tramore's first Listed race, was introduced on New Year's Day 2005 and was won by Cloudy Bays, a consistent horse who has also won a Grade 2 chase at Leopardstown and the Troytown Chase in Navan. Sue Phelan managed another coup on this day by persuading Michael Hourigan to bring Beef Or Salmon to parade, fresh from his victory over Best Mate in the Lexus Chase (Group 1) during the Leopardstown Christmas racing festival.

* * *

Action from Tramore

Tramore is an amazing track. It has only four flights of hurdles on a circuit, there are no sprints and there are no starting stalls, either. It has really sharp inclines and descents, and a corner with a guiding wall that is padded with foam which has prompted Paddy Graffin, clerk of the course, to say, 'If you can keep a horse balanced round here, Epsom's easy.' Talking of the Epsom Derby, Tramore was used as a dummy run in 1983 when trainer Liam Browne gave his Epsom candidate a post-racing gallop the *wrong* way round the course, so that his colt, Carlingford Castle, could get a feel for left-handed gradients in advance of the real thing. It nearly paid off, too, Carlingford Castle finishing a far-from-disgraced second to Teenoso.

Paddy Graffin rode just short of 200 winners during his amateur career, was several times leading point-to-point rider in the North and once tied for the whole of Ireland championship. He won 11 races with a horse called Kilnantogue, including the Soudavar Champion Hurdle at Down Royal.

His is one of those faces you are likely to see on many far-flung Irish tracks, for he doubles up as clerk of the course, judge, starter, stewards' secretary, clerk of the scales and inspector of courses. This is the way it is done in Ireland among the Turf Club officials, many of whom are retired jockeys, so that anyone going racing can be assured that the officials understand

Paddy Graffin, clerk of the course at Tramore – and Wexford, and Gowran Park – and that's just for starters . . .

every facet of racing, Paddy is clerk of the course at Tramore, Wexford and Gowran Park, but he can also be seen starting up in Downpatrick, or as a stewards' secretary at courses as far apart as Cork and Sligo, Punchestown and Tralee. Luckily he now lives in Co. Laois in the centre of Ireland.

Tramore is truly a 'horses for courses' track, and among its past specialists have been Audity, Dariole and Garvivonnian, who made a habit of winning at Tramore most times they ran there. Garvivonnian is a splendid servant to owner-breeders Mr and Mrs John Long and trainer Edward Mitchell. He has run 78 times to date, travelling to all parts of the country from his Kilmallock, Co. Limerick, base. He keeps appearing in Ireland's prestigious handicap chases, such as the Irish Grand National at Fairyhouse, the Troytown at Navan, the Kerry National at Listowel (he was fourth there in 2005) and the Galway Plate. But it is at Tramore that he excels – three of his ten wins have been there, and he was runner-up on his only other appearance at the Waterford venue. To recognise these specialists, Sue Phelan has introduced a Racehorse of the Year award, based on an individual horse's performance on the course, and the inaugural award was presented at the 2005 August Festival to Dariole, who has won at five consecutive Tramore festivals.

* * *

The annual highlight of Tramore, or to give it its full title, Waterford and Tramore, is its four-day festival in mid-August which ties in with Waterford City's festival. Thousands of tourists flock to both. The picturesque city of Waterford on the River Suir, home to the Waterford Crystal glass factory, is only eight miles away.

A number of racegoers join the throng late, and all of them stay late – and why not, for there is a brass show band playing in front of the main stand, and there are numerous places to eat and drink. The festival marquee serves barbecue meals all day and for those inclined to stay put the racing can be viewed on television. There is Tote betting on site, too. For those watching from the stands, there is also a big screen. One jockey took advantage of it, looking across to see how far clear he was on the run-in. The answer was far enough, so he had no need to resort to the whip.

Tiered steps that allow a good view of the paddock are always packed. Shirtsleeves and sunhats mingle with a handful of ultra-smartly dressed women. Yes, it's Ladies Day, the Saturday of the Thursday-to-Sunday meeting; and, just to be fair, there's a Most Stylish Man competition too.

The races are three hurdles, a chase, and three flat races. Some of the visitors barely realise what races are on, they are enjoying themselves too much with their friends, but for many more Irish it is studious scrutiny of the form and serious interest in the racing, with or without a bet. For holidaymakers and punters alike, Tramore has a real festival flavour in the summer and is a great way to see out the old and bring in the new with its two-day New Year's Eve and New Year's Day meeting in the winter.

TRALEE

As the visitor heads south-west and reaches the southern border of Co. Limerick expansive views unfold before him across the northern part of the Kingdom of Kerry. It is a vista that entices him to come further and sample the region's numerous delights, all the while watched over by Macgillycuddy's Reeks. It is only half an hour from here to Ballybeggan Park on the edge of the city, the ninety-seven-and-a-half-acre stonewalled former deer park that is home to Tralee races. The park was once home to Daniel O'Connell, known in Ireland as 'the Liberator', for his work in emancipating Catholics, assisting the poor and the building of national schools during the late eighteenth and early nineteenth centuries. The Liberator Handicap is run each year on the Sunday of the course's June meeting.

Back in the nineteenth century there was a stallion called Daniel O'Connell who covered a mare in Co. Kerry called Mary O'Toole. This liaison produced The Liberator. The Liberator won his first race in Cork Park and then the Galway Plate of 1875, and in 1879 he won the Aintree Grand National. He had fallen in his first attempt and finished third in 1877; he was also second the year after his victory, carrying 12 st. 7 lb (compared with 11 st. 4 lb when he won). He tried again the next two years, remounting to finish ninth in 1881 (still on 12 st. 7 lb) and, again humping that

Pointing the way at Tralee races

weight, he fell once more the following year.

First records indicate racing in Tralee dating from 1767 and although its venue was changed several times it soon gained a good reputation. It moved to its present home back in 1889 and has remained there, bar a gap in the 1930s and '40s, until 1946, when the Ballybeggan Park Company bought it. It was this innovative company that introduced the now world-famous Rose of Tralee beauty contest in the late 1950s as part of the racing festival and which attracts some 100,000 people from many parts of the world. Nowadays many will be watching the event on television. The Rose is selected on the Tuesday evening and she attends the Wednesday of the races. That famous song,

Everywhere there are colourful flowers and throngs of relaxed racegoers

'The Rose of Tralee', is older, having been penned in the mid-nineteenth century by William Mulchinock.

There are only two meetings a year at Tralee, but what meetings they are: three days in early June, followed by the International Rose of Tralee Festival meeting, covering four days in late August.

* * *

My initial impression warrants the term 'festival' and this is soon confirmed: everywhere I look there are banks of colourful flowers and throngs of relaxed racegoers obviously in holiday mode. It rains so hard during the morning of my visit that the day's sport has to first survive an early-morning inspection, but it is clear that enthusiasm has not been dampened for visitors, such as a couple with their little baby from Co. Louth (just about diagonally opposite Tralee).

'We love going racing,' they said, 'from here we'll go on to Ballinrobe.'

Hard work from the team behind the scenes plays its part in creating the atmosphere, of course, and here continuity is the key: Denis Switzer, for instance, began by helping with the racecards 50 years ago and nowadays carries out many of the office duties, while Alan Casey has also been supervising the turnstiles, gates and staff for close on a half-century since the festival began.

It is a day for the family and locals, as well as visitors from afar among the crowd of between 5,000 and 10,000. It is local

A young visitor from Co. Louth

success on the racetrack, too. The handicap hurdle springs a surprise: top weight is Paddy Mullins's well-regarded Hurry Bob, and then comes Cloudy Bays, more familiar to chasing aficionados. But the winner is the 8–1 chance Owennacurra Bobby, who relishes the heavy ground. Being stabled with Tom Cooper only ten minutes away at Farmers Bridge has also ensured little stress in travelling. The gelding had been bought three years previously as a yearling at Tattersalls (Ireland) sales and this is his first win, in the hands of leading amateur N.P. Slippers Madden.

In action at Tralee

'He's been unlucky and I hoped he might win, especially as he likes soft ground,' Tom Cooper admits. Tom, in his early 40s and a dental technician by trade, took out a permit in 1990, following in the footsteps of his late father, Des. It was only in 1998 that he took out a public licence to train.

* * *

It is with the wonderful mare Total Enjoyment that Tom has made his name, and it was after a rather good night out among friends that she was purchased for €20,000, with him cannily keeping one share for himself. She was bred by Kerry-born Noel Collins, who lives in Mullingar, Co. Westmeath, and she was by an American stallion called Flemensfirth out of a Bustino mare. From

the beginning she showed herself a mare with tremendous guts. Shared by a group of Kerry businessmen, mostly from Tralee, they rather forebodingly called themselves the It Will Never Last Syndicate. After an initial third place in the Punchestown Festival bumper, she won at Fairyhouse, after which the sporting owners wisely turned down big money for her. Another win at Leopardstown was followed by the most prestigious bumper of them all at the Cheltenham Festival in 2004. There, she completed her hat-trick in the hands of fellow Kerryman Jim Culloty.

Afterwards, Tom admitted to the press that she 'was a nutcase when we were breaking her and she used to regularly throw off lads. I've been lucky to have a few decent horses, but nothing like her. She could be anything.'

Guiding the talents of a good mare the right way, as Tom had clearly done, results in one, like the little girl with the curl, who is very, very good. She was Tom's first-ever runner at Cheltenham and the celebrations, naturally, continued well into the night. When she made it four in a row on her hurdling debut the next season at the Down Royal Festival, the world looked her oyster, prompting her trainer to say, 'She's a flying machine. She winged the first hurdle and after that she was on her way. She's the sort of horse which nothing fazes.'

Naturally, there were hopes for Cheltenham, but two baffling unplaced runs followed and Tom wisely gave her a bit of a holiday, turning her out by day in a field. 'Dr Green', as grass is known, is an excellent tonic. But disaster struck.

Tom Cooper takes up the story, 'I was walking round the gallop when I noticed her standing by the gate, which was unusual early in the day. She must have then turned round and attempted to jump the 6-ft fence beside the gate; it had a 5-ft drain beyond it, and then a stone laneway.'

When Tom got there, the mare had landed in a heap at the far side and injured a knee so badly that her life was in danger for some days. She stayed in the Troytown veterinary hospital in Kildare for nine weeks, returning home near the end of March 2005. 'At least we have her

The finish

saved as a brood mare,' Tom had said, 'and if she's ever able to run again, it will be a bonus.'

But the end of April brought the devastating news that she had had to be put down.

Another famous mare with a Tralee connection was Dawn Run, who not only won her initial bumper there in June 1982, ridden by her 63-year-old owner, Charmian Hill (the very day she was informed her riding licence would not be renewed), but also returned that September to give Tom Mullins, the youngest member of the famous family, a resolute success beating 15 subsequent winners.

* * *

Back at the Rose of Tralee Festival meeting, Ciara's Surprise lives up to her name, winning the maiden hurdle for owner/trainer Jarlath P. Fahey, who trains with his brother, Seamus, at Monasterevan in Co. Kildare. The jockey is Pat Fahey. There are happy scenes in the spacious winners' enclosure afterwards.

That the festival is able to survive four days of racing after continuous heavy rain is due to good work by the management team, headed by chairman Paddy Barry and general manager Timothy Griffin, who ensure that there is new ground each day for horses to run on.

Tralee has been a course with a question mark over its future – the land is worth a mint for development – but its Tim Griffin is reassuring. 'It is in no more danger than any other course,' he asserts.

DOWNPATRICK

If Tramore is steep and unusual (which it is), wait until you visit Downpatrick. Unique could be misused here, but there is surely only one Downpatrick. Think funfair switchback ride. And if you're about to ride in a flat race, make sure you don't end up facing a steeplechase fence – yes, it has happened!

It is a marvellous track to visit: very pretty, small, quiet, intimate. In the centre is a working farm and fields grazed by cattle and sheep. The three-mile chase start is steeply uphill. Trains used to pause here to allow passengers to watch proceedings through the windows. If passengers wanted to get off, they had to wait until the train pulled into the platform behind the stands.

* * *

Back to the three-milers. As they reach the summit after starting, the runners turn sharply right-handed before encountering the first fence. It gives the impression of jumping into outer space, but the horses jump it well. Walking the course, there are lovely views from here of hills and woods, and back across to the stands, the town church in the distance. They say that when you can see the Mountains of Mourne, rain is on the way; when you can't, it is already raining.

Walking (or racing) on, we come more gently downhill to the two-and-a-half-mile start where the course is very narrow. So narrow that it seems almost inevitable that a horse is kicked at the start. It is Ruby Walsh's mount, and the starter checks he is all right before calling them in again. No wonder the maximum number of runners allowed in any one race is only 15, there is simply not room for more to be spread across the course. The jockeys vie for position, some of them trying to jump the gun, and there is a false start. But Paddy Graffin, the starter, is having none of it; he is getting quite stern. One jockey is warned that if he 'tries it on again' he will be reported to the stewards.

Ruby Walsh had shown all his expertise earlier when landing the maiden hurdle on Right Jack for delighted trainer Pat Fahy, who'd travelled up from Co. Carlow.

'Ruby's hard to get, but when he's been available, he's won on five of his last eight rides for me,' he enthuses. 'This horse has been all over the country trying to win a race, but Ruby gets on him and he wins by half the track!'

There is a fairy-tale ending to the two-mile two-furlong Joe Rea Memorial Handicap Chase. The bottom weight, Fernhillbogey, has been off the course for more than three years since pulling up in a chase at Killarney in July 2001 and had finished plumb last in two hurdle races a year before that. His only previous win had been in Kilbeggan in July 1999, and he had been through several trainers' hands. But in Colman Hennessy, who

came all the way up from Co. Cork, he had a patient, as well as astute, owner–trainer. Claimer John Allen took another 5 lb off his back and with three of the principals falling, the 20–1 twelve year old went on to a seven-length victory.

The course rises up towards the winning post and then disappears. It simply drops away in sharp descent before continuing its switchback ride up, down, then steeply up again to where we began at the three-mile start. The story goes (and it's been verified) that once the then apprentice jockey Keiren Fallon and two others found themselves jumping the steeplechase fence at the bottom of the steep chute after the finish.

Originally the course used to continue into the far distance. That was back in 1685 when it was the Down Royal races. The court was in Downpatrick town a mile away, so the people would watch a hanging in the morning and then go racing in the afternoon. Eventually the court was moved to Maze. A new course was built on the current Down Royal site, and the Down Hunt held its point-to-point at Downpatrick. Recently the course has been undergoing a steady refurbishment: a new weighing room was built in 1997, thanks to the stalwart supporters' club that was founded in the early 1970s, and in 2000 a new stand was built with a lottery grant, funding from Horse Racing Ireland, by selling corporate boxes and through the

Downpatrick racecourse resembles a switchback ride. Here (after the finish line) it drops away in a sharp descent

Not much room at the start

129

Bookmakers at Downpatrick: they do a brisk trade at all Irish meetings

course's own funds. In January 2005 work began on building new stables on the racecourse side of the increasingly busy main road, which will be much safer than their current situation.

Only one and a half miles away is where Brave Inca was foaled on Denis McCaulay's farm. Brave Inca had been unplaced in two hurdle races, including behind Kicking King at Naas in 2002, but then won two bumpers and five hurdles in a row. His seven-race sequence culminated in winning the 2004 Supreme Novices Hurdle at Cheltenham by a neck, and in an even closer finish at Punchestown, winning by a short head. It was a wonderful season for the sporting Novices Syndicate and trainer Colm Murphy,

though they were to see the other frustrating side of close finishes the next season when it was four seconds in a row, one by a short head, and third in the Champion Hurdle, beaten a neck and a neck. He finally, and deservedly, triumphed at Punchestown in April.

Looking back to an earlier age, Caughoo, victor of the 1947 Grand National, won at Downpatrick. Bred in Fethard-on-Sea, Co. Wexford, he was sold as a two year old in Ballsbridge sales for £50 to vet Mr Herbert McDowell for his brother, J.J. McDowell, a Dublin businessman. Caughoo became something of a Downpatrick specialist, winning the National Handicap Chase there in both 1946 and 1947, so it is somewhat surprising that his starting price at Aintree was 100–1. Perhaps it was because there were 55 runners. He became, at eight years old, one of only three 100–1 winners of the Grand National (Tipperary Tim and Gregalach in 1928–29 were the previous 100–1 winners, and in 1967 Foinavon became the fourth). It is said that his Co. Meath rider, E. Dempsey, had never been to England before, let alone ridden over the Aintree fences.

Dual Irish Grand National winner Rhyme 'N Reason, who also won the Aintree Grand National (1988) and placed in the Cheltenham Gold Cup, began his racing career here. Others who have gone on to success at Cheltenham include Sparky Gayle and Rathgorman.

Downpatrick holds the Ulster National in late February/early March, a race that trainer Arthur Moore won as a rider on Copper Kiln VI for Willie Rooney in 1972. In 1980 he also trained the winner, Champerty, ridden by Mick Ennis at the age of 42, and he worked for Arthur's father Dan.

Downpatrick can take pride in its record, which includes being one of only four courses where all the races are sponsored, something like seventy in a year. Hat's off to them.

* * *

The name Fitzsimmons is synonymous with Downpatrick, as was the family's grey horse, Bright Trick, who won many races here in the late 1960s and early 1970s. The late Frank Fitzsimmons was born in the farmhouse in the middle of the course, rode as an amateur and trained a small string. He rode alongside the likes of Bunny Cox, Francis Flood, Tim and Martin Molony and Billy Rooney on horses such as Major T.W. Hughes's Copper Ridge and Copper Cottage, and he won 17 point-to-points on Bright Trick. His two eldest sons, Brian and Frankie, also won on him, having first hunted with the East Down, showjumped, Pony Club'd, shown ponies and ridden out on the racehorses, as their younger brother, Paddy, was to later on. By the time Paddy came on the scene,

The grey Bright Trick in his heyday on 'his' course

Bright Trick had retired, but Brian won three races on him in 1971, two hunter chases and a handicap chase, all of them at Downpatrick. Frankie also won on him at Downpatrick, as well as finishing third there in the Ulster National.

'He wasn't a good traveller,' Brian Fitzsimmons recalls, 'but at Downpatrick he could be back in his box ten minutes after running in a race. We used to put a radio on in the stable so that he wouldn't hear the other races being run within 100 yards of his box.'

Bright Trick was by a French show-jumping sire called Paniko, but he also sired successful racehorses Inishargie and The Molar (owned by two dentists), who was favourite for the Grand National one year when trained by Josh Gifford.

Living on the course meant that the family of riders and the horse himself knew the ground intimately and knew exactly when to press the button or where to take a pull. Talk about horses for courses!

Since then Brian, a retired civil servant, has now been a steward on the course for 30 years, is a member of the Turf Club, was the first steward of the Turf Club from Northern Ireland and, at the local point-to-points, will do whatever job is asked of him, putting something back into the sport which has given him so much.

He recalls his first-ever race-ride, in a bumper at Down Royal in 1964 in a field of 33. He weighed 7 st. 9 lb and had to carry 11 st. 9 lb, which he managed with a 21 lb suede saddle and lead. 'The saddle was like an armchair and gave tremendous grip when it was wet,' he remembers.

His grandmother, Mary, owned one-third of Downpatrick racecourse, and it is now in the hands of his cousins. He remembers Major Beamish, who used to train nearby, and says that Dermot Weld 'always brings flat horses to start here'.

SEPTEMBER

LAYTOWN

It is low tide and three miles of golden sand stretch out below the sand dunes. A wonderful place to gallop on, the wind rushing past, the little waves breaking, the hooves pounding like drumbeats, reverberating the ground, echoing in the air. Sandpipers and seagulls fly out of the way. And up ahead are the white plastic running rails and temporary winning post, and there is a little crowd gathered on the sand dunes.

Unique. That much overused word. But not in the case of Laytown, a small seaside resort in Co. Meath on the east coast of Ireland just 29 miles north of Dublin. Most courses rely on the weather, Laytown depends upon the tides. It has to be low tide to run at Laytown, the only official races held on a beach anywhere in Great Britain or Ireland, and probably the world.

It's a one-day meeting held in May, June or September – the high season of July and August has been avoided since a distressing accident in 1994, of which more in a moment.

* * *

The day I visit, the meeting is about as Irish as it's possible to get, right down to the story that it was a priest who organised the first meeting back in 1876. Today no one seems to know whether that is fact or fiction, but it's good entertainment anyway. The races were held intermittently until 1901 when the landowner, one Paddy Delaney, established the meeting that has been run ever since (bar once) come hell or high water!

Imagine a race meeting for which the track cannot be prepared until the morning of the race. At Laytown it is all systems go from dawn, as soon as the tide turns and begins its outward journey again, revealing this stretch of sand. The work involves scuffing the sand with a seaweed machine – harrowing would be too dire – erecting running rails over the last furlong on the seaward side and chestnut paling to hold back spectators on the landward side. The whole length is flagged and each start distance is marked and provided with a starter's rostrum. The damming of surface water is undertaken in strategic places to prevent water channels appearing across the course.

The little three-acre field above the winning post can be prepared a few days earlier; the tents are erected to become temporary changing and weighing rooms, an office for the stewards and the secretary, bars and restaurants, and portable loos – surprisingly smart ones for the ladies. There are no stables and so the runners are prepared inside their horseboxes, just as at a point-to-point. The area is roped off, providing a basic form of security, and both the organisers and the Turf Club provide security guards. White railings enclose the paddock, and its centrepiece is a garden table and chairs surrounded by colourful pots of flowers, with the trophies displayed on the table. Bookmakers, the usual high number of them, erect their pitches, and there is also a tented Tote. There are permanent concrete steps up to the top of the dunes.

Sadly in 1994 there was a bad accident. There were huge crowds milling around on the beach, where many of the attractions were also located, the hurdy-gurdies, the ice-cream vans, even the betting. In those days the whole width of the low-tide sand was used to create a horseshoe course for the longer races. The straight sprint race was held first, giving extra time for the staff to work on the longer course as the tide receded. The bend in the horseshoe was more like a hairpin, but it had been like that for years. And, as it turned out, had nothing to do with the accident, as this occurred in the first race, a sprint for which there were about seven runners. Usually the horses would jump the little channels that in places crossed the course, but on this occasion the leader knuckled over, bringing down half the field with him. More than one horse was killed and two of the jockeys were seriously hurt.

Unbelievably, another accident happened the same day. There were about 100 mounted marshals, many of them from the local hunt. One of the ponies bolted and collided with a runner at the finish. Jockey Robbie Burke suffered a broken leg, and it was not until 2003 that he rode again at Laytown, with a great result, winning the third race on Mrs P.D. Osborne's Love, trained by R.J. Osborne.

If Laytown was ever to be held again after that terrible year, drastic safety measures had to be taken. The manager/secretary, Joe Collins, now a senior Irish clerk of the course, put several proposals to the Turf Club. Since then, no three year olds have been allowed to run; only a straight course may be used; no blinkers are allowed; there is a maximum of ten runners per race; the races are not to be held in high summer in case of crowd problems; beach attractions are banned from the strand and most of the spectators are to remain within the enclosure round the dunes; and with no crowds on the beach, there are no mounted marshals either.

The 2002 meeting had to be called off at the last minute, when everyone was there, because of storm water that kept appearing across the track from the new housing developments along the coastline. This was a problem that put the 2003 meeting in jeopardy for an anxious few days beforehand, due to a similar problem at the mile marker.

The solution was to abandon the longer-distance races and divide the three remaining six and seven furlong ones to make up a six-race card.

I was intrigued to notice a few days before the 2003 meeting that there were many entries from Ted Walsh. I thought of him more for jumping and at the smarter

Going to the start

The start

135

Sheltering from the showers

tracks, though like most trainers he holds a dual licence and is just as capable of producing winners on the Flat. And, with Ireland's minimum-value policy, it means that even these sand races are run for prizes from €9,000 to €10,000.

Many people arrive by train from Dublin; drivers park their cars in a field in the village a mile away, and their occupants are conveyed to the races by a fleet of shuttle buses. The day is more like an April one, cool sunshine interrupted by heavy showers, some with hail and strong winds. But everyone is in holiday mode, more than 2,000 of them, many in shirtsleeves, and they are greeted, as ever, at the entrance by the band of ladies selling fruit and chocolate. Be it Leopardstown or Laytown, they are there.

Inside, someone is hiring binoculars. 'Who wants to see the horses?' he calls.

Before long the runners for the first are parading, and the bookmakers are doing a brisk trade. The stewards and judge make their way to their respective eyries, and the commentator to his, only to have his notes blown out of his hand and into the garden of the bungalow next door. A racegoer retrieves them; luckily the race hasn't started yet. The races are competitive, and one of them produces a dead heat for second place; well, there's no permanent winning line here and that's much the fairest decision. So the minor spoils are shared between Vijay and Indian Desert, while the first prize goes to the five-year-old Love in the fairy-tale comeback ride for Robbie Burke.

Down at the three-furlong marker a machine is pumping water away to prevent an unwanted channel from carving its way across the race stretch. Thankfully it succeeds. There is a delay before the start of the second race, but luckily nothing more serious than that some of the white plastic railing has blown down in the wind.

What a race it turns into. Scooting home at 11–1 is Kid Creole in the hands of Ruby Walsh – and now I discover the reason for all those entries. With this victory, Ruby has won on every Irish racecourse, something a flat jockey cannot achieve because Kilbeggan is for jumping only.

* * *

Ruby Walsh was born to ride.

His father, Ted, was always going to be an amateur – and some amateur at that, with 600 wins, more than anyone else in either Ireland or Britain – but Ruby, with his lighter build, his will to win and eagerness to learn, became the youngest ever NH professional champion jockey of Ireland at the age of 19 – and he had been champion amateur at 17, again the youngest ever, and at 18.

Walsh involvement in racing has always been a family affair and it remains so today. Ted's record as a trainer is of the highest; his wife, Helen, is not only a sound back-up but owns some of the horses, too. Ted junior, not of a jockey's build, is more of a rugby player and lends moral support; Jennifer is Ruby's agent, a time-consuming job in itself, and also a TV presenter, and Katie, who, as a young teenager, was praised by her father for being a highly talented rider of whom more may well be heard, is proving that prediction and is riding winners.

At only 25, Ruby is a senior rider, a horseman as well as a jockey. He puts much of this down not only to the tuition he grew up with, but also from his spell with Enda Bolger when he was starting off. Enda frequently sent him hunting in Limerick and that's what put the horseman into the jockey; that and some pretty firm verbal advice from the cross-country king.

Ruby nowadays spends much time

Some of the railings have blown down before the start of the second race

Ruby Walsh: winning at Laytown in 2003 meant he had scored at every track in Ireland

commuting between riding in England and home. He was offered poll position for the highly talented Paul Nicholls' stable in Somerset, but, like his colleague Paul Carberry, he prefers to live in his home country. Here in Ireland he rides principally for Willie Mullins, as well as his father. Ruby is a hard-working young man 'with a brain', who lives for racing and has been rewarded with some top successes.

It wasn't easy the whole way. Every jump jockey endures injuries, but in October 1999 Ruby was particularly unfortunate. He'd been flying, with wins in the Heineken Gold Cup at Punchestown on Imperial Call and in the Galway Plate on Moscow Express, earlier that year. In the Czech Republic, preparing to ride Risk Of Thunder in the Velka Pardubice, the Czech Grand National, he rode first in one of the warm-up races to get a feel for this twisting course and its wide variety of obstacles. On the way round he collided with a piece of broken running rail that was jutting out. It speared his shin, embedding itself in his leg. Racing at 30 mph, an accident like that inevitably spells disaster: not only was the leg broken, but the flesh was also badly torn. After three months on the sidelines, Ruby started riding out at home. He took another tumble, and the injury on his leg reopened, sidelining him for a further two months.

He missed the winning ride on Micko's Dream in the Thyestes Chase at Gowran Park in January and reckons that, had he been able to ride him then, he might well have opted for him in the Aintree Grand National. But that ticket went to Jason Titley, so Ruby, back into race-riding barely a month after five months off, teamed up with his father's Papillon, owned by American Betty Moran, for the 2000 Grand National – and went into the record books as the first winner of the new millennium in the world's greatest NH race. (Just for the record, Micko's Dream fell at the first.)

Two weeks after that, Ruby was in the winner's enclosure at the Irish Grand National, this time with former Austrian Derby winner Commanche Court, and then again with the same horse in the Heineken Gold Cup at Punchestown.

Over in England his steady stream of winners have included the Whitbread Gold Cup twice with Ad Hoc, the 2004 Queen Mother Champion Chase with Azertyuiop and two Festival winners in 2005: the inaugural running of the *Daily Telegraph* Chase over two and a half miles on Thisthatandtother and the Champion Bumper on Missed That for Willie Mullins.

Ruby won the first three of the four domestic nationals in 2005, a remarkable achievement in itself, and then came within half an inch, literally, at the end of the four-mile marathon trip in the last national of that season. He had won the Welsh National on Silver Birch, the great Aintree event on Hedgehunter and the Irish equivalent on Numbersixvalverde. Three weeks later he was on the enigmatic Cornish Rebel, a full brother to Best Mate, for the Scottish version – and went down by literally a whisker, the judge taking several minutes to announce his verdict after close scrutiny of the photograph.

Any horse ridden by Ruby Walsh, no matter what the event, is guaranteed a good ride from the man on top.

* * *

Back to Laytown for the 2004 meeting. There was, with the benefit of hindsight, an intriguing runner in one of the seven-furlong events. By Sadler's Wells out of an Irish Oaks-winning mare by Rainbow Quest, he was certainly bred to stay further and could, perhaps should, have been of Derby class. As a yearling he was sold for 460,000 guineas, but as a flat racer in England at three years, he was an abject failure. His four unplaced runs included being last of eight in a £5,000 maiden at Pontefract.

So it was back to the sales. Enter Kildare agency Emerald Bloodstock, who purchased him for 8,000 guineas (less than most point-to-pointers), a drop of 452,000 guineas in two years.

The bay, who to some bears similarities to Istabraq, went to Naas trainer Michael O'Brien and into the BPS syndicate. He won his first two hurdles in big fields at Down Royal and Fairyhouse, came third in a €48,000 hurdle at the Punchestown Festival in April, and reappeared in August in a flat race at Gowran Park, finishing second.

He was then gelded, which can knock a horse back a bit, so his wise trainer decided a trip to the seaside might perk him up, as with many a convalescent. He couldn't win at that Laytown trip, of course, and finished sixth of ten; but it did the trick mentally; sweetened him up.

For it was none other than Essex, the horse who went on to win the Irish Cesarewitch on The Curragh and then his next two hurdle races: the prestigious Pierse Hurdle at Leopardstown, followed by the totesport (formerly Schweppes) Hurdle at Newbury in England; with that, Essex earned his place in the 2005 Smurfit Champion Hurdle line-up. He ran a cracking race being close on the heels of Hardy Eustace for much of the way, but gave way to more experienced runners in the end. Age – and a talented trainer – is on his side.

That summer of 2004 may have marked a turning point for Laytown races as well, when about 200 spectators made their way onto the beach, prompting one local lady to say it was 'just like old times'.

These people had reached the beach by ways other than through the turnstiles into the enclosure; if they wanted to access the facilities within the enclosure from the beach, they would be faced with a fence and gateman, ensuring that they would have to pay to go in. Then along came a paid-up visitor from *inside* the enclosure

Starting young

asking that gateman how much it would cost him to gain access to the beach . . .

It is a scenario that current manager/ secretary Kevin Coleman understands well, having grown up in Laytown. He can remember searching for gaps in the fence as a little boy, so that he could gain access . . . In those days there were crowds right across the course at the finish, parting like the Red Sea only moments before the runners swept through. It is the work of people like Kevin Coleman and chairman Niall Delany, who is from a long line of family support for the meeting (seven Delanys currently serve on the enthusiastic committee) that ensures the future for this unique fixture in the Irish calendar.

LISTOWEL

Listowel. The Kerry National. A seven-day festival in September run by an octogenarian.

Listowel is yet another of those special Irish places, famed for its literary connection and the spirited annual racing festival. It is a real one-off.

The first thing that hits you is the festival atmosphere throughout the town, and then again among the huge crowds on the course. It is the day of the Kerry National. Last year it was so dry that hundreds of gallons of water were pumped on to the course from the river. This year it is wet. Very wet.

The track, like others, is so close to the town that much new development has gone up nearby, but at Listowel there is a difference: the course is on the other side of the River Feale. To gain entry visitors have to walk over a narrow bridge, almost like a drawbridge over a moat.

It only has two meetings per year, one during the May Bank Holiday weekend and then the festival in September. This is when the farmers have gathered in their hay and finished their harvest, and can relax for some days at the races. They come from all over the island of Ireland.

This meeting began in 1858 as a two-day fixture and it has gradually increased over the century and a half since, in line with its continuing popularity. It became three days in 1924, four days in 1972 and five in 1977. In 1992 it extended to six

days, and ten years later it joined only Galway in becoming a meeting of seven consecutive days. Brendan Daly, secretary for 55 years and 80-something young, explains, 'We used to be five days, Monday to Friday, then we added the Saturday, and about four years ago the Sunday.'

'But Sunday is now the first day?' I ask.

'Only this year,' Brendan explains, 'because if held on the following Sunday, it would clash with the All-Ireland Gaelic football final. When we were planning the fixture, we hoped that Kerry would be playing in it.'

And they are. Against Mayo. Listowel will be like a ghost town, all the streets and towns and villages within the county of Kerry will be empty. Those who have not been able to make it to Croke Park, the purpose-built showpiece GAA stadium in Dublin, will be glued to televisions in their homes or local bars. (For the record, Kerry won.)

Brendan, whose daughter, Brenda, is assistant secretary, was born, bred and reared in Listowel. An accountant in the town, he never rode but was always interested in racing, in the horses rather than the betting – 'just a little flutter occasionally' – but he mainly wanted to see how the horses were doing.

Preparation for next year's meetings begin the day after this one closes. The land lies unused in-between, no grazing, no events, no functions, just tended when necessary by a groundsman.

Brendan Daly, the secretary, assisted by
his daughter Brenda

'I've seen many changes here in half a
century,' says Brendan, 'but the greatest of
all has been in the prize money. It used to
be £3,200.'

'For the Kerry National?' I ask.

'No, for the whole meeting.' He adds,
'Now it's €1.2 million.'

Because the course is non-profit-
making, it is able to plough everything it
makes back into the course, one year a new
yard, another new stables, then a sponsors'
bar; next in the pipeline is a restaurant. 'It's
a bit like farming,' he says. 'It's never
finished.'

Outside, the steady rain of earlier has
eased to the sort that somehow just creeps

into your elbows before you've realised it's
happening. Three flat races are followed by
a hurdle, then the Kerry National, another
chase, another hurdle and a bumper to
conclude.

As the runners go out for the second, a
seven-furlong handicap, there is a flashy
chestnut filly misbehaving, throwing
herself about all over the place. She would
have dislodged many a jockey, but this one
sits like a limpet, even managing a
reassuring pat as the filly, called Summer
Magic, finally settles to canter to post. She
is second-top weight, but the form
comment reads, 'needs to improve if she is
to have any hopes of success'.

Luckily Summer Magic hasn't read that
and she wins the race for trainer Timothy
Doyle and owner Mr J. Stephenson. And
who was the jockey who sat tight, calmed
the filly and then rode the race with such
good effect? Catherine Gannon, who was
to go on to become Ireland's first-ever
female Champion Apprentice at the end of
that season.

Cathy Gannon has been like a breath of
fresh air in Irish flat racing. She has a
lovely open smile and sparkling green eyes.
An incredibly hard worker, she is aiming
all the time to improve, with a goal of
riding in the big races. She was born on
Dublin's north side, with three brothers, in
an environment in which a number of
horses and ponies virtually ran wild
around the housing estates. She learnt to
ride bareback and mucked out her

brothers' ponies while they were away running trotters at Portmarnock. She idolised Johnny Murtagh and American ace Julie Krone, but with no racing contacts of her own, it was thanks to her schoolteacher that she was put in touch with RACE, the apprentices' school on The Curragh, in 1996 when she was 15. Of the six girls on the course, which was as much about discipline and responsibility as riding in a race, only she and one other saw it through.

Even after, when she moved on to John Oxx, she wasn't allowed on a racehorse for a year, but rode three ponies. Finally, in 1998, she had her first race-ride in public, on Bayyardi at Wexford, and finished third – but then fell off past the post and again when she unsaddled, so fatigued was she from all the 'pushing and shoving' involved in riding a finish. Never let it be said that a jockey just sits there! It is incredibly hard, physical work, and the toughest part comes near the end, just when you might be tiring as well as your horse, for then the rider has to try and hold the horse together and galvanise it to produce every ounce that it's capable of – and then some more. It is not only the physical effort, for the rider's wind must be clear as a whistle too. All this comes with preparation and practice, but the first race will always be the hardest.

Catherine gained her first win on Quevilly at Tipperary, but she achieved only a few in the early years – one year produced

Cathy Gannon, 'a breath of fresh air in Irish flat racing'

just one win from seventy rides – then a cracked vertebrae saw her out of action for three months. But Catherine was not for quitting. She came back to finish second in the apprentices title of 2003, and then clinched it in 2004, bringing with it numerous awards, not only in racing but also as Ireland's first Sportswoman of the Year, which she received from the President of Ireland, Mary McAleese.

Before long she will be riding on level weights with her heroes. With the effort she puts in, listening and learning, she deserves to succeed all the way to the top.

* * *

Back at Listowel on Kerry National day. Over the next few races, the ups and downs of a jump jockey's life, even those at the top of their game, are thrown into perspective. Paul Carberry rides an

Kerry National-winner Banasan
(Ruby Walsh)

Top-weight Barrow Drive (Jim Culloty)

144

exceptionally clever race, as only he can, in the first hurdle on No Half Session for Noel Meade, but is then on the deck in the next two. For Ruby Walsh it is a similar story: he wins the big one, then falls in the next.

The Kerry National lives up to its name and reputation, sponsored by Guinness to the tune of €150,000. Among the big field of 16 are several with lively prospects. Could top-weight Barrow Drive carry 12 st. successfully in this heavy ground for trainer Tony Mullins and jockey Jim Culloty? By contrast, Howaya Pet is carrying only 9 st. 5 lb and has won his last two races, both staying chases. Paul Carberry's mount, The Culdee, is considered to have chances and is fit from running on the Flat.

Veteran trainer Joseph Crowley has two in the field: Golden Storm has won his last two and has speed and stamina, while Fatherofthebride has possibilities. Then there is Banasan, out on a retrieval mission when favourite, but only sixth on much firmer ground than this at Galway in the Galway Plate.

By the time they canter down to the start the ground is clearly very heavy; after one circuit the field is depleted and those that remain are already plastered in mud. Barrow Drive puts up a really brave performance, but in the end his concession of a stone to Banasan, beautifully ridden by Ruby Walsh, and of 2 st. to Fatherofthebride, proves just too much.

Only six of the sixteen finish, the other three being Garvivonnian, Splendour and Howaya Pet.

So it is off to the winner's enclosure for Banasan, rider Ruby Walsh, trainer Michael O'Brien and owner S. Mulryan. Ruby slips off to weigh in, and then weighs out again for the next, while for the owner and his friends it's a visit to the hospitality room.

Here Louise Harrison is hospitality hostess. She takes care of the winning connections after every race with free drinks and pleasant smiles. The little bar is tucked away at the end of the office buildings, and Louise definitely doesn't see any racing from here, not even on a television.

'We don't have one because sometimes it can be a little bit difficult to get one lot of winning owners out before the next lot come in,' she explains. 'I haven't seen a race in the four years I've been here, but it's a lovely job because everyone who comes in here is happy at having just won a race. But occasionally it is tricky to get them out again, especially big syndicates!'

'Listowel revolves around its week-long festival,' she continues. 'Not much else goes on, though the seaside resort of

Hospitality is served up to happy winners by Louise Harrison (in the background)

Ballybunion is popular, especially for its bachelor festival, and, of course, there's interest in John B. Keane, the writer and playwright who came from Listowel.'

Keane, who died in 2002, also owned a pub in the town, which is now run by his son, Billy, and is still known simply as John B's.

It is evident that Listowel loves its festival, and the festival depends a lot on the people of Listowel. It is a fitting finale to the summer round of racing festivals.

145

CLONMEL

From the moment of walking through its smart entrance, the atmosphere at Clonmel greets the visitor. Directly ahead is a live two-piece band and to the left the immaculate paddock. Its centrepiece is a large, mature yucca tree, its palm-like fronds swaying over the attractive shrubs around it. The paddock is enclosed by a thick, smartly trimmed hedge, with tall trees at the far end.

My first sight of the attractive, park-like course was enough to make me yearn for my racing saddle: it looks a lovely course to ride round, a large oval of one and a quarter miles. It has a steep uphill on the short side bounded by tall firs, a wonderful gallop along the top beside a line of poplars and then a long, sweeping downhill curve taking horses well into the home straight,

View of Clonmel racecourse, also known as Powerstown Park

where the final stretch is a challenging climb uphill. It is a testing course with a respected reputation.

It is set in wonderful scenery, with the foothills of the Comeragh Mountains behind the stands, the mighty Slievenamon over to the north, and the whole set in the valley of the River Suir.

The two stands are separated by the bookmakers' pitches set out in a big horseshoe arrangement. Beyond the second stand, parallel to the last two flights of hurdles, is the row of racecourse stables, so although these are, of course, secured behind high wire, visitors can, if they wish, watch from the stand as horses are washed down after their exertions, an unusual feature because at most courses the stables are tucked well out of sight.

Walking the course it is obvious that a lot of care is taken with it. Uniformly green and well mown, even the couple of road crossings have had grass cuttings sprinkled over the lightly coloured shavings, so that a racing horse will neither be startled nor try to jump the width of them.

Although at first glance it would appear that the 160-acre centre of the course is simply used for grazing agricultural animals, it has another use: this is the site of the national coursing championships. Coursing figures greatly in the life of Clonmel general manager Jerry Desmond, which is probably what brought him from running a bonded warehouse in Cork to the job here.

That was in 1986. Jerry is currently on

the board of Horse Racing Ireland, where he is chairman of the media-rights committee and is therefore deeply involved with SIS (who broadcast odds and beam live viewing of races to bookmakers worldwide) and *At The Races*; he is also chairman of the Association of Irish Racecourses. In addition, he is secretary of the Irish Coursing Club and Keeper of the *National Stud Book* in which he registers about 20,000 pedigree greyhounds every year, from about 4,000 litters. Every one has to have ear tattoos.

Jerry also deals with the owners and, for good measure, edits and manages the weekly *Sporting Press* newspaper devoted largely to greyhound racing and coursing. 'Yes,' he admits, 'I look at the racing as a relaxation.'

But that does not mean there is anything amateur about it. Clonmel, also known as Powerstown Park, clearly has first-class management with top class sponsored races, beautifully cared for grounds and a loyal local, as well as national, following.

The regulars are catered for with their own supporters' club, founded in 1988 and run by chairman Tom Bourke and secretary Cecily Purcell, while at the time of my visit the indefatigable Maurice Dougan, a vet and pharmacist, was president. Sadly he died in the spring of '05. Cecily's family has bred many wonderful NH horses, not least Champion Hurdler Gaye Brief and the great hunter chaser Eliogarty.

Clonmel holds meetings virtually throughout the year, staging 12 fixtures in

View from the stand to the last flight, with the stables on the right

all. Its biggest race is the Clonmel Oil Chase (Grade 2) held in November. It always draws some of Ireland's best chasers and sometimes from further afield. In 2003 it was won by the great veteran Edredon Bleu, who, like Best Mate, is owned and trained by Jim Lewis and Henrietta Knight in England, until his retirement in August 2005. The owner/trainer combination tried again with Impek in 2004, but this was Rathgar Beau's much-deserved day. He had been beaten by the likes of Beef Or Salmon, Moscow Flyer and Kicking King, and in his most recent run had been the only one who could conceivably challenge Moscow Flyer in a chase at Navan when he spectacularly ejected his jockey, Shay

Barry, at the last fence. He made no such mistake this time and, held up early by Shay Barry, challenged coming to the last and held on well from Cloudy Bays.

By Beau Sher, Rathgar Beau is owned by a sporting group of men who met in a pub in Rathgar, Dublin, and formed the One O Eight Racing Club. At least one member is a car dealer because I bought my Jeep from him! Trained by Eamon 'Dusty' Sheehy, Rathgar Beau went on to win the Hilly Way Chase in Cork, ran uncharacteristically badly in Leopardstown (under the ace Tony McCoy), but two more wins, in Thurles and Gowran, earned him a tilt at the *Daily Telegraph* Chase at Cheltenham. In this he finished third to Thisthatandtother, bred here in Clonmel by Mrs Joerg Vasicek. In April he beat none other than Moscow Flyer in a titan duel at Punchestown.

Past Clonmel Oil Chase winners have included Beef Or Salmon, but the biggest crowd puller was Dorans Pride, who won this race four years in a row from 1997 to 2000. His story is told in Ballinrobe.

Racing at Clonmel has an intriguing history. During the nineteenth century, and just into the twentieth, admittance was free and open to all, but in 1913 the owner, Villiers Morton Jackson, enclosed the course and put it on to a commercial footing. He confined bookmakers to their own set area. He must have felt there was a need for it to clean up its act as he banned gaming sideshows, brought in detectives and police to deter pickpockets and then somewhat unscrupulously charged two shillings (10p) a head for entry into a roofless grandstand capable of holding 1,500.

Clonmel is one of many Irish racecourses to have benefited from considerable refurbishment in the late 1990s. This has included a new grandstand with bar and eating area, a computerised turnstile entrance and a refurbished weighing room and jockeys' room. The evening meetings sometimes include barbecues, in December a number of Christmas parties are held, and there are various sporting fundraising events. The course centre is also the site of game fairs, Pony Club events, dog shows and caravan rallies.

* * *

During my visit in September, the card consists of three flat races, three hurdles and a bumper. It is good racing and the Dermot Weld–Pat Smullen combination win the first with Monaser for Hamdan Al Maktoum; Rory Cleary takes the apprentice claiming race for trainer Timothy Doyle with Laoise Beag. P.T. Gallagher, claiming 7 lb, takes the three-year-old maiden hurdle with Onforatwist for owner/trainer Frank Lacy from Ballycrystal Stud, Geashill, Co. Offaly. By Courtship, the filly was bred there by Edward Lacy. There were some close finishes and friendly, welcoming people, and the viewing here is excellent.

I left looking forward to next time.

OCTOBER

TIPPERARY

Umbrellas. Macs. A smiling Barry Geraghty, fresh from winning the Grand National on Monty's Pass, greets us strangers cheerfully as we park side by side. It is a late June meeting in Tipperary, one of several held regularly from April to October, and, as usual, it is a mixed card.

My friend has a share in a two-year-old filly, Tashadelek, making her debut in the five-furlong maiden stakes. Fellow co-owners are met, and we are all introduced to the trainer, Pat Flynn, and then the jockey, the late Timmy Houlihan, who tips his cap before being lifted lightly onto the little chestnut's back.

She runs well enough to finish fifth, but is no match for the winner, the Aidan O'Brien-trained Day Of The Cat. Second is Blue Crush, a chestnut filly bred by Willie Robinson, forever remembered as Mill House's rider. Blue Crush became a regular at Tipperary in the summer of 2003, winning two races and then finishing second in a Listed race.

* * *

Tipperary might look small, set beside a railway with its station that is still called Limerick Junction, even though it is just outside Tipperary town. The races used to be called Limerick Junction as well, until the name changed to Tipperary in 1985 because too many visitors were turning up at Limerick city, fully 24 miles away. The

Istabraq

Slievefelim Mountains form a backdrop to the course when they are not lost in cloud. The track itself has a reputation for nurturing future Classic horses, Hawk Wing and High Chaparral among them, who both won their maidens here.

It is only a few miles from the Ballydoyle stables, near the historic, ancient town of Cashel, made famous by Vincent O'Brien, and now successfully run by his namesake but no relation, Aidan O'Brien.

The centrepiece of Tipperary's year is its concluding meeting known as Super Sunday, and with genuine reason, since it features the John James McManus

Memorial Hurdle (Grade 1) and the Coolmore Stud Home of Champions Concorde Stakes (Group 3). 'The best mixed card in Ireland,' manager Peter Roe proudly proclaims. Six of the eight races are named after former Tipperary favourites: Danehill Dancer, the champion Irish juvenile of 1995; High Chaparral, who won his maiden here at Tipperary before going on to win both the Epsom and Irish Derbys of 2002, back-to-back wins in the Breeders Cup Turf and finally, gloriously, the 2003 Irish Champion Stakes.

Grimes's name was attached to the Kevin McManus Bookmaker Novice Chase, worth a healthy €45,000, but the 11 year old ran in the feature hurdle, of which more in a moment. Joe Mac, who died after only seven runs, but won four of them, had his name on the Kevin McManus Hurdle (Grade 3). Time For A Run (after whom the handicap hurdle is named) and Mucklemeg (the bumper) were both trained in Co. Tipperary by Edward O'Grady and both won at the 1994 Cheltenham Festival.

* * *

That first Sunday in October is a sporting one both locally and internationally and, aware of this, racing from Longchamp for the Prix de l'Arc de Triomphe is shown in one bar, and action from the golf at Mount Juliet and the final of the Irish women's football were shown elsewhere in the enclosure. There was also the ubiquitous best-dressed lady competition. And, of course, both Istabraq and Risk Of Thunder paraded before the feature hurdle for all to admire – and remember their glory days. This is a race Istabraq won three times.

The place is buzzing, the crowds are great and the day lives up to its billing, not least in the John James McManus Memorial (Grade 1) two-mile hurdle worth €100,000. Even with the withdrawal of Ansar and Royal Alphabet, it is an intriguing quartet that is left: Accordion Etoile, Grimes, Harchibald and Solerina. Solerina is the toughest of little mares and a confirmed frontrunner just like her illustrious stable companion, now retired, Limestone Lad. From the three or four horse restricted permit stable of the Bowe family on the Kilkenny–Tipperary border, these two between them have won more than fifty races. But can she beat Harchibald, fifth in the previous year's Vincent O'Brien County Hurdle at Cheltenham and tipped as a Smurfit Champion Hurdle horse for next time? And then Accordion Etoile, winner of the €60,000 Betdaq.com Hurdle at the Tipperary July meeting, has a band of followers as a course and distance winner.

Before the race Istabraq and Risk Of Thunder show off their well-being to the crowds, and in the race Solerina makes all and never sees another horse. Accordion

Solerina, winner of the €100,000 John James McManus Memorial Hurdle

Etoile beats Harchibald for second place, with Grimes in fourth.

In Peter Roe, Tipperary has an enthusiastic young manager dedicated to keeping the track open. He had been assistant trainer to John Dunlop in England and then was assistant manager at Fairyhouse. When he came to Tipperary in 1999, its lease was about to end and the track was threatened with closure. A committee of local supporters, for whom Peter Roe works, managed to negotiate a three-year reprieve, later extended to five years.

'Schooling is the main thing that keeps

us going,' says Peter. 'We have about 1,500 horses gallop here during the winter, and we have a number of schooling bumpers. Total Enjoyment schooled in one of those.

'The supporters, including Timmy Hyde as chairman, plus Tommy Stack, Danny O'Connell, various point-to-point people and local businessmen, invested about a half-million and no one takes a penny out. The place was bad structurally, for example the windows were dilapidated, the drainage was poor, the ambulance road needed improvements and the first-aid room needed doing up. We had some grant aid too, and the place is basically tidy now, but the supporters want to keep on developing it.

'We attract good horses here, such as Yesterday, Hawk Wing, High Chaparral, Back in Front, Intersky Falcon and Solerina. Aidan [O'Brien] likes the track and brings his two year olds to race here, like In Excelsis.

'People will come to watch nice racing, not rubbish, so we always look to stage at least one race that will attract the customers to us.'

* * *

It is the local track for J.P. McManus, and he attends whenever he can. Forty years or so ago J.P. was a JCB driver. Employed by his father, Johnny, he helped in the building of Martinstown Stud, Co. Limerick, for June McCalmont, from the generations-old racing family of Mount

Juliet fame. Today Martinstown is J.P.'s home, and has been since 1982.

In-between J.P. had taken out a bookmaker's licence at 21, made his colleagues quake when he wanted his own money down (all too often limited to safeguard their satchels, especially at Cheltenham), turned to gambling on financial markets where limits were not imposed on the amount he punted, and become a partner in the renowned Sandy Lane Hotel, Barbados.

But Martinstown is about much more than J.P.'s Irish home or money. It is about this legendary gambler's hobby: racehorses, in particular the rearing and resting and retirement of them. Between times, they are distributed among a number of talented trainers on all sides of the Irish and English channels to show their paces and win their races, or not, as the case may be. Whatever, there is always a home for them at Martinstown; one field alone is designated for former Cheltenham winners.

Then Istabraq and his constant companion Risk Of Thunder, the expert banker, are in the field behind the current house, close at hand to show guests. It also keeps them handy for their regular tours, Istabraq being in constant demand for parades, Risk Of Thunder, 'The Boss', going along for the ride. Both horses are kept semi-fit for such engagements by daily bouts on the mechanical horsewalker.

There are four hundred acres here at Martinstown, housing four separate yards,

Istabraq (left) and Risk Of Thunder at home

each with its walker. All of it is in prime Scarteen Black and Tan hunting country.

'Yes, we are hunt friendly,' says farm manager Tom Russell.

The horses that spend their summer holidays here all go back to their respective trainers fit enough to start cantering on their return. There are also 200 head of beef cattle, immaculate post-and-railed fencing, many young hedges and trees growing, plus new stonewalled bridges across the drainage ditches. The Galtee Mountains overlook the fertile plain one way and the hill of Knocklong another; all the horses are stabled in the winter and the yards have all-weather turn-out arenas for use in the wet months.

On my visit two famous horses are in, slowly preparing for their return to racing:

the enormous and highly talented mare Like-A-Butterfly, and Le Coudray. Both have been fired (for tendon trouble) in the past, which prompts Tom Russell to say, 'If our vet says six months' rest is needed for a horse, we give it twelve.' Then confesses the 'we' is a euphemism for J.P.

Like-A-Butterfly won her first eight races from January 2001 until March 2002, when she was beaten for the first time at the Punchestown Festival. But another win when she reappeared in January 2003 entitled her to an (unsuccessful) appearance in Rooster Booster's Champion Hurdle, followed by a third at Aintree, at which point J.P. announced she would go chasing the next year.

But heat in a tendon, followed by the

The Cheltenham retirees, Elegant Lord (one of J.P.'s favourite horses) on the right, turned out at Martinstown Stud, J.P. McManus's Irish home

firing operation and the crucial long rest at Martinstown, meant it was a year and a half before she ran again. It was her first chase, she is a big, big mare and she had been off 19 months, but in former champion flat jockey Christy Roche she had a first-class trainer. He produced her fit and well-schooled to win on her chasing debut at Naas in November 2004, in the competent hands of Conor O'Dwyer. She pulled up at Leopardstown and was beaten into fifth in the Royal & SunAlliance Novice Chase at Cheltenham, but she came back to take the Powers Gold Cup at Fairyhouse at Easter 2005. She was 11 years old and winning a Grade 1 novice chase.

This big mare with masculine qualities,

which remind one of Dawn Run, won again at Aintree in April, in the gamest fashion. Afterwards J.P. said, 'She's in very good hands with Christy; we thought about retiring her after Christmas, but then she started showing a little spark. He loves her more than anything; we all do.'

Like-A-Butterfly did not run until she was seven years old – another example of the patience J.P. is prepared to give to a horse. Le Coudray's comeback following his fall in the 2004 Grand National was less successful, being unplaced in Leopardstown and pulled up in the Irish Grand National.

As I continue my tour round Martinstown, we come to a field where Youlneverwalkalone is grazing. He sustained a spiral fracture of his cannon bone in the Aintree Grand National. Another field is reserved for retirees, all of whom, bar one, have won at Cheltenham: the grey Blitzkreig, Khayrawani, Lucky Town, Front Line, Time For A Run, Elegant Lord, Rith Dubh – only Wylde Hide among them never raced outside Ireland, but as a dual winner of the Thystes he has earned his place with them. When their racing days are over, all of them have a home to return to.

J.P. has a special soft spot for Elegant Lord, the chestnut who ran in nineteen hunter chases and one chase, winning thirteen of them, eleven with Enda Bolger in the saddle, including a seven-timer and the 1996 Cheltenham Foxhunters, beating Cool Dawn. He ended his career with

the magnificent Foxhunters double, Cheltenham and Aintree, in 1999, ridden by Philip Fenton.

Health alone, or rather the decline of it, is what decides when a horse will be put down; in 2004 that decision was made for the mare, Cilldara, who, at a mighty 33 years old 'just wasn't blooming'. A much-loved hobby to J.P., the horses are well cared for, neither spoiled nor neglected, in their old age.

J.P. is a quiet, unassuming, pleasant man for all his business acumen and accumulated millions. He has gathered around him a loyal and enthusiastic staff, often giving youngsters a chance.

Tom Russell, whose uncle bred Rheingold, says, 'My very good assistant is John O'Brien. The ethos is in leading, not driving; it's a good crew in a happy ship.'

A total of 40 are employed on the farm and in the state-of-the-art offices that are set between the house and the main yard, and its 100 acres. The remaining three yards and three hundred acres are on the other side of the road, and this is where much improvement work has been carried out, not that anything can be done to make the winters dryer, hence all the yards.

A missionary from a particularly poor area of a trouble-torn African country once made a visit and some of the staff were afraid all the evident wealth would be an anathema to the man. Far from it. 'It is good to see

J.P. McManus in the rain at his local track, Tipperary

money being spent,' the missionary said, 'and, with it, all the employment and other good things it brings.'

Money is something that J.P. has made huge amounts of, but he remains a reserved man with an engaging smile and a passionate love of National Hunt racing. As a philanthropist he gives not only to racing's needs, but also to other things as wide apart as his local GAA county board or the 2004 tsunami disaster. He does these things quietly, not courting publicity, and there will be many more such gestures the public will not know about.

ROSCOMMON

Roscommon is one of the prettiest racecourses, and I loved its summer-evening atmosphere from the moment I arrived. It is only a 'minor' course, having just nine meetings between April and October, but it is clear that the management, under Michael Finneran, puts in a lot of effort. For one thing, every race is sponsored locally – 'So we consider every race a feature race,' he says.

In October 2005 Roscommon is due to stage the €40,000 Kilbegnet Novice Chase (Grade 3) at its final meeting of the season, and in 2004 it deservedly won the Stable Staff Award for the most improved racecourse in Ireland. This followed a similar award in 2000 from the Racing Club of Ireland. 'So, now we have had that

accolade from both the punters and visitors coming into enjoy themselves,' a delighted Michael Finneran, says, 'and from the industry staff who come here as part of their work.'

The tiny paddock has a beautifully manicured lawn and pristine flowerbed, and there are two long lines of bookmakers, their umbrellas up shielding them from the sun, not rain! Shirtsleeves and casual dress are the order of the day.

The surrounding farmland is dotted with gorsebushes in full golden bloom and the stone walls that are indigenous of the area. Sheep and single-suckle herds of cattle graze the land and overhead the swallows swoop in search of early evening insects. The town of Roscommon can be seen in the distance and is dominated by its church; beyond the far end of the course there is a gentle line of hills.

The land is jointly owned by the racecourse and the coursing club, so when it's too wet in winter to race, it's used for coursing. Everything about this venue is sporting.

Racing began here in 1837, when there was a British garrison in the town, and with the exception of a period between 1936 and 1948, it has been in use ever since. The course is a long, fairly narrow oblong with some undulation, and although the bends are fairly tight at each end, it has long galloping stretches down both sides.

Michael Finneran, chairman Dick

Long rows of bookmakers

O'Brien and vice-chairman Shane Fleming are proud of some of the top flat and NH horses who have run here, especially Imperial Call, trained by the legendary, now retired Fergie Sutherland in the mid-1990s. He went on to win the 1996 Cheltenham Gold Cup in the hands of Conor O'Dwyer.

Imperial Call won sixteen of the thirty-two races he contested and was placed in a further nine. A dark brown, he ran some marvellous races. As a five year old he was beaten a short head by Dorans Pride in a hurdle race at Naas. He had already won four of his seven starts over hurdles before Roscommon was chosen as the venue for him to make his debut over fences. Ridden as he was in most of those early races by Gerry O'Neill, he finished a promising third in a field of 11 novices on the last day of Roscommon's season in October 1994. The crowd had been treated to a glimpse of a future star, for Imperial Call not only won the Cheltenham Gold Cup, but also chases in front of his home crowd on many occasions in Punchestown, Limerick, Naas, Clonmel and Leopardstown. But Roscommon is quite rightly proud that they saw him first as a chaser.

Roscommon also saw an emerging flat star in the form of the John Oxx-trained Enzeli in August 1998 when, at odds-on and ridden by Johnny Murtagh, the three year old by Kahyasi easily accounted for his five rivals in the one-and-a-half-mile race. In June 1999, less than a year later,

View of Roscommon

Enzeli became the first Irish horse for thirty years to win the coveted Ascot Gold Cup over two and a half miles. He had sixteen rivals that day and was again ridden by Johnny Murtagh – this time his starting price was 20–1 – beating Invermark by one and a half lengths.

* * *

On the evening of my visit, racing begins with four flat races, followed by two steeplechases, one hurdle and a bumper. There are no sprints, three of the flat races are over a mile and a half, and the other a mile and a quarter. There is a splendid husband and wife double for jockey Pat Smullen and trainer Frances Crowley.

Evening sunlight at Roscommon

Pat wins the second race, a maiden, on board the Dermot Weld-trained Russian Tsar for joint owners Seamus Sheridan, Michael Smurfit, T.A. Ryan and Donald Keough – Pat looks as happy and smiling to be winning that as for a Group winner on a major track.

The next, a handicap, brings a neck and short-head finish and some drama when a horse runs out left-handed for the paddock on the first bend, plunging into the railings, knocking over a course photographer and unseating his girl jockey who has been slapping the horse down its left shoulder to try and keep him on the course. Luckily all concerned get up unscathed.

The first steeplechase is run in memory of Frank Hannon, late father of Roscommon committee member Oliver Hannon (part of four Roscommon joint owners of dual Cheltenham winner Montelado). The race is won by Iggy Madden's Wests Awake in another close finish, as are most of the races, adding to the evening's excitement. Finally, the bumper winner is trained by Frances Crowley, Pat Smullen's wife, and ridden by promising claimer Tom Cleary.

* * *

Roscommon has seen many top riders, owners, trainers and horses, including 2005 Cheltenham hero Tom Taaffe. In a professional riding career that lasted 12 years, Tom won at every Irish track, not least Roscommon.

As I write in 2005, he will go down to posterity as trainer of the Cheltenham Gold Cup winner, Kicking King, exactly 40 years after the second of his father's three wins riding Arkle, and 31 years after Pat himself trained Captain Christy to the same pinnacle.

Arthur Moore, one of the gentlemen of Irish racing, gave Tom Taaffe his first ride as a jockey, just as Dan Moore had done for Pat Taaffe. For many Irish racing fans, Tom's father was a superstar. At home, near Straffan, Co. Kildare, Tom remembered Pat being humble and a man of few words, 'but when he did say something, if you listened, you learnt. He was renowned for these qualities throughout the Turf, and his only interest was horses.'

Pat was well known as a rider before Arkle – he had already won the Grand National on Quare Times in 1955 (and was to do so again in 1970 on Gay Trip). He married Molly Lyons, one of two sisters and five brothers (one doctor and four vets). The eldest, Bill, was in Cheltenham for all of Arkle's victories and was there again in '05 for Kicking King's.

Pat Taaffe died in July 1992, having gained an extra year of life – and his retirement pastime of horses – before rejection set in following heart surgery. 'The doctor told him he would never ride again, but after about five months Pat said life wasn't worth living if he didn't,' recalls Tom, whose mother died two years later.

On the day of my visit to Tom's home, a week after the memorable Gold Cup – before which Kicking King looked a picture of rude good health, a lean, fit athlete – he showed me the gallop that goes up the only hill in the area, right past the veranda of his ultra-modern house near Straffan. The house is ingeniously designed and that day resembled a train station (normal, with two young sons, Pat and Alex bouncing around) and a florist's shop, as yet another bouquet of congratulations arrives.

Tom and Elaine's first son, Pat, was born the day Kicking King won his first race, prompting the thought, can Pat

The Taaffe home and training grounds

Tom, Pat and Alex Taaffe

159

emulate his father and grandfather, and might Kicking King rival Arkle?

Meanwhile, Tom had a more important appointment. He promised Elaine that should he win a race in Cheltenham, then he would marry her, a pledge he fulfilled a few months later.

'Well, I've always been unconventional,' he admits.

Tom has the ideal owner in Kicking King's Conor Clarkson. 'He's a friend and has had horses with me for a long time; he has a great passion for racing and his best attribute is he's as good a loser as he is a winner.

'Most of our owners are hand-picked, and all are of that nature.'

NOVEMBER

DOWN ROYAL

There are two courses in Northern Ireland and in type Down Royal and Downpatrick are like chalk and cheese, or little and large. Down Royal's circuit, at nearly two miles, is one of the longest in Ireland, a real galloping track that produces an excellent festival in November; Downpatrick's is short, sharp, tight and very steep.

The two courses share a common foundation, both claiming to have hosted their first race in 1685. In fact, it was at Downpatrick that Down Royal races began, organised by the military, and was moved to its current site at Maze, near Lisburn, when the military moved there in 1789. The old Down Royal course at Downpatrick then became Downpatrick, if you follow the logic.

So the two meetings can be seen jointly as the oldest in Ireland. The claim to the Byerley Turk having run belongs to Down Royal, though the venue for this famous battle-charger and progenitor of the modern thoroughbred was, of course, Downpatrick, over its then three-mile horseshoe-shaped course.

Horse racing originated in ancient times when it was popular in Arabia. There was horse racing in the early Greek Olympic Games (though chariot racing was more popular), when there was both prize money and sponsorship. Earliest records for the Olympic Games go back to 776 BC

– when the all-male participants were naked; women were not allowed at the Games in those days. The Romans introduced racing to Britain in about AD 210 (at Netherby in Yorkshire). Racing in Roman Britain was seen as having such a high status that certain individuals were keen to donate cash to the meetings, so enabling them to climb the social ladder – and thus became early sponsors.

The Romans, of course, never succeeded in invading Ireland. But when flat racing became popular at Newmarket, England, there was one Irish nobleman, Sir Edmund O'Brien, 2nd Baronet of Dromoland, who enjoyed it so much that he renamed his Co. Clare village Newmarket-on-Fergus and laid out a racetrack on his land at Turret Hill. Racing on The Curragh is said to date from prehistoric times, and there are records dating from Norman times.

It was from Arabia and Turkey that the three stallions who founded the thoroughbred horse arrived in the West: the Godolphin and the Darley Arabians, and the Byerley Turk. The *Stud Book* today goes back to these three foundation sires, dating from the mid-seventeenth to early eighteenth century. Racing was already taking place, of course, and as early as 1565 one Thomas Blundeville was advocating breeding along the best bloodlines. The sport was patronised by James I and Charles I during the early part of the seventeenth century, and Newmarket became established

as a racing centre, with trophies put up by the King. In the mid-seventeenth century, along came Oliver Cromwell to ban horse racing (along with far more dire actions). He kept breeding horses for his cavalry, however, and by the time Charles II was on the throne in 1649, there was regular racing on a dozen courses including Newmarket and Epsom. More Oriental stallions arrived to influence the budding racehorse, but of one hundred and three original Oriental stallions registered in the *Stud Book*, only the three mentioned above have continued their lines down the centuries.

The Byerley Turk was a spoil of war, captured by Captain Robert Byerley during the siege of Vienna in 1683; he was taken to Ireland where Captain Byerley, a close aide to King William III of Orange, rode his import in the Battle of the Boyne in 1690; before that, probably whiling away the time before battle, he had already run at Down Royal. Even so, little could Captain Byerley have guessed at the value of the horse flesh beneath him when he then sent him to stud in Yorkshire. His influence as a sire is still felt today, via Jig first of all, then his grandson Partner, who was the best racehorse of his day around 1718. There was then Herod, or King Herod, in 1758; Diomed in 1777; The Flying Dutchman in 1846; and the spotted grey The Tetrarch in 1911 – great racehorses and sires all of them, all descended directly from Byerley Turk.

The Tetrarch was bred at Mount Juliet in Co. Kilkenny by Dermot McCalmont, who in turn bred Tetrama, who was the sire of Dermot McCalmont's Thyestes, after whom the famous chase in Gowran Park is named. Following Byerley Turk's line still further, his later descendants include Tourbillon, Levmoss, Luthir and, in 1966, Blakeney, who won the 1969 English Derby.

The Down Royal Corporation of Horse Breeders was created by Royal Charter of James II in 1685 to encourage the thoroughbred breed in Co. Down. Five years later, with the Battle of the Boyne looming, his rival, William III, was persuaded to grant £100 for a plate to be raced for annually. Sixty years later, King George II added another £100.

Down Royal course is only ten miles south of Belfast, close to Lisburn and the A1 trunk route between Belfast and Dublin. It holds its popular two-day Northern Ireland Festival of Racing in early November, featuring the James Nicholson Wine Merchant Champion Chase. This invariably tells the race-going public about the well-being of last season's leading heroes and throws up potential new ones, with Cheltenham the following March in mind.

In local man Mike Todd, the course has a progressive young manager, and one who was born into horses. His first ride in a bumper was here at Down Royal, as were

Swimming is part of the fitness routine at Michael Hourigan's. Beef Or Salmon shows his prowess (top) and then dries off in the sunshine (below). The James Nicholson Chase at Down Royal in November 2004 saw him account for subsequent Gold Cup-winner Kicking King

Media Puzzle, owned by Sir Michael Smurfit, won the Millennium Ulster Derby at Down Royal two years before his victory in the Melbourne Cup

to enjoy it. Other improvements include a new weighing-room complex.

It should be noted, however, that Down Royal hosts both the Ulster Derby and the Coolmore Ulster Oaks on the Flat. The inaugural running of the Ulster Derby in 1936 was won by Black Domino, owned by American William Woodward and trained by Captain Cecil Boyd-Rochfort. The Millennium Derby in 2000 was won by the Dermot Weld-trained Media Puzzle, who two years later went on to win the Melbourne Cup in Australia.

* * *

both his hurdles and steeplechasing debuts, as an amateur rider. He is also working towards holding a full trainer's licence. It is clear that for him holding the Down Royal post is something to which he was born. He took up the role in 1996 and since then has concentrated on maintaining the track in tip-top condition, with the help of course foreman Carson Lyons and his team.

'My other main aim is to put on races that the public want to see, which up here means as much jumping as possible,' he says. 'Our sort of racegoers are likely to use a flat race as an excuse to go off for a drink.' When they do, they will find a newly painted main public bar in which

As I walk round the newly widened track on the second day of the festival, a group of Japanese golfers wave cheerily and continue with their game, seemingly oblivious to the horse race going on around them. Golfers are briefed in advance of the race times.

The fences are beautifully prepared, *à la* Cheltenham, and take up the outside of the track, a thick hedge marking the outer boundary much of the way. Two ponds in the course centre look pretty, though I suspect they are there more for hazards to the golfers than as an attraction for racing spectators. A newly surfaced road runs round the inside of the course and has its convoy of about five vehicles (officials, medical, veterinary etc.) during every race, as at every other course nowadays. The ground looks in great shape, helped, no

doubt, by the acquisition of a vertidrainer that breaks up compaction.

The first day ensures the festival gets off to a bright start with horses that are to confirm their star status later in the season. The brave Brave Inca, victor of the opening Supreme Novices Hurdle at the previous year's Cheltenham Festival, fails to concede 10 lb to another rising star, Macs Joy, in the Anglo Irish Bank Hurdle. This is the first of what was to become three defeats of Brave Inca by Macs Joy that season, one of them by a short head. Both horses are shortly to become two of the seven top-priced Irish runners for the following spring's Smurfit Champion Hurdle – Brave Inca, a neck and a neck third behind Hardy Eustace and Harchibald, had Macs Joy behind him on that occasion.

For the Scarvagh House Stud Mares Maiden Hurdle (Grade 3) on the same card there is victory on her hurdling debut for the previous year's Cheltenham Festival Bumper winner, Total Enjoyment, the lovely mare trained in Co. Kerry by Tom Cooper.

Course specialist Dawadari makes it three out of three at Down Royal in the Archie Watson Memorial flat race under 7 lb-claimer Keith Bowens. Trainer Stephen Mahon is quick to cite Cheltenham as the main aim.

If Cheltenham, four months hence, is on many people's lips on the Friday, it is even more so the next day, when several

Racing at Down Royal

Irish heroes are declared for the James Nicholson, headed by Beef Or Salmon.

The previous year's winner, Glenelly Gale, trained by Arthur Moore, is in the line-up, as is Munster National-winner Colca Canyon, representing Jessica Harrington, and the Troytown winner, Cloudy Bays, a confirmed frontrunner. The consistent Harbour Pilot has the added assistance of Paul Carberry in the saddle, while attempting three miles for the first time is the promising Kicking King.

In the race Cloudy Bays leads as usual until Kicking King takes over with two to jump, and it looks as though a turn-up might be on the cards; but Timmy Murphy usually bides his time on Beef Or Salmon and then uses his superior speed at the end. He does so again and joins

The old stand, packed for the November Festival

Kicking King at the last, then forges ahead up the straight.

Owned locally by Joe Craig and Dan McLarnon, there are some present who feel his win is not convincing enough, yet runner-up Kicking King was only a few weeks later to win the King George at Kempton and become a leading contender for the '05 Cheltenham Gold Cup. Not only did he win steeplechasing's feature, but he stamped his superiority by winning at Ireland's NH festival at Punchestown in April. A feared bug had put his Cheltenham participation in doubt, but as we now know, a convincing win from the seven year old was in the offing, while Beef Or Salmon, come the day, was the one found to be ailing.

* * *

Beef Or Salmon has had an unorthodox career. Three times the sale fell through before his current owners purchased him from Michael Hourigan. Joe and Dan were visiting the yard at Lisaleen near Patrickswell, Co. Limerick, with Seamus McCloy, who told Michael Hourigan they wanted a horse. They had travelled all the way from Co. Antrim, they wanted some craic and it was p***ing down with rain.

'They might as well have this one behind me, then,' Michael said. 'He'll win on Sunday.'

They went into the house to discuss the unfashionably bred chestnut and over a cup of tea a deal was done: £30,000, plus £5,000 for his first point-to-point win and the same amount for his first bumper victory.

At the point-to-point that weekend at Dungarvin, 'Salmon' was well clear when he over-jumped at the last and came down, but next time out, near Clonmel, he won by the proverbial street, ridden by Davy Russell; he was passing the winning post before any of the other runners had even reached the last fence. Likewise, he also won his second bumper, under Philip Fenton.

Joe and Dan have proved model owners, leaving the trainer to train the horse, but enjoying the craic with him whenever they meet up, be it at home or on the racecourse.

Of the three who pulled out on agreed deals, of £10,000, £12,000 and £15,000 respectively, they can only rue the day. One prospective purchaser had apparently discovered what Michael had paid for the horse at the sales and decided he was expecting too much profit. No matter that since the sales the horse had been re-broken, schooled and brought on patiently, and shown himself to be 'a good un' in the making.

In fact, Michael had taken quite a chance in purchasing him in the first place. The story was that the horse was back at the sales for a second time, the original purchaser having found him 'impossible to ride'.

Beef Or Salmon's first bumper appearance was at Fairyhouse in May 2001, when he was third of 27. He then had his summer holiday and didn't run again until Clonmel the following November when he 'hacked up'.

Paul Hourigan rode him in his first hurdle race when, two strides after jumping the last, he slipped and fell. He then won another bumper under Philip Fenton before Paul won a flat race on him in Gowran Park in January 2002.

The following October he took part in another flat race, at Galway, this time with Laura Hourigan in the saddle, and the pair won convincingly. After one more run in a flat race (and only two, unplaced, hurdle races), Michael Hourigan then took a very brave decision.

The horse was schooling over fences at home in scintillating fashion and had already won a point-to-point. The 'normal' route would have been to run

Fence maintenance during a meeting at Down Royal

next in novice chases and then probably to progress to handicaps unless showing exceptional ability, in which case he could contest the sport's top chases at level weights.

Novice chases, by their very nature, can see a number of fallers, and these might impede or even bring down other runners; some will run 'green' and wander off a straight course, causing interference. A top open chase, by contrast, will be contested by just a handful of seasoned, talented campaigners who are unlikely to cause such problems, but will, of course, have much more experience and speed than most novices. Salmon was not only schooling well at home and on racecourse schooling sessions, but he had already shown the speed to win on the Flat. Michael Hourigan went straight for a Grade 2 race, the Clonmel Oil Chase, valued at €21,000, in November 2002.

He wasn't wrong in his assessment. Ridden by Paul Carberry, he beat none other than Sackville, who had at that time won the first 16 of his career total 18 victories. It was the first public hint of things to come.

Timmy Murphy took over for most of Salmon's remaining NH runs, winning the next three; again, not just any old races, but the Hilly Way Chase (Grade 3) in Cork and then two Christmas and New Year crackers, the Grade 1 events in Leopardstown on 28 December, the Ericsson, now Lexus Chase, and the Hennessy Cognac Gold Cup on 9 February 2003, beating Colonel Braxton and Harbour Light, two of the country's leading chasers at the time, in both.

It was enough to warrant a crack at the Cheltenham Gold Cup, no less. There were inevitably those who declared it a year too soon, but the same had been said of Dawn Run when she went for her Gold Cup with only four chases behind her.

So it was on 13 March 2003 amid much English/Irish hype between the holder, Best Mate, and the young pretender, Beef Or Salmon, that Salmon took his place in the line-up. The crunching fall he took at an early fence, somersaulting not once but twice, could so easily have been fatal. Although not immediately apparent, it left a legacy of back problems that took months of patient remedial work to put right. Liz Kent worked on his back, and in the saddle, performing dressage exercises, was Sue Shortt. All the while he was cared for by Kay Hourigan, his devoted 'lass', and the Patrickswell team. And yet, amazingly, only three weeks after that fall Beef Or Salmon won a 28-runner flat race on The Curragh, ridden by ace flat jockey Mick Kinane.

The winter of 2003–04 saw Salmon beaten in the Clonmel Oil Chase by the rejuvenated veteran of that year, former Queen Mother Champion two-mile chaser Edredon Bleu. Beef Or Salmon then beat first Tiutchev at Punchestown in the John Durkan Memorial Chase (Grade 1), then Rathgar Beau in the Hilly Way at Cork. There were then further defeats on his home ground at Leopardstown by Best Mate in the Ericsson, and in the Cheltenham Gold Cup, where, nursed to jump the bigger track, he ended up a fast-finishing fourth behind Best Mate. He ended the season back in the winner's enclosure at the Punchestown Festival by again taking the John Durkan Memorial; it was John Durkan who found and first trained Isabraq only to have his young life cut short by a debilitating illness.

The next season began, as we have seen, with Beef Or Salmon beating Kicking

King in the James Nicholson at Down Royal. I doubt if many predicted that day that Kicking King would win the Gold Cup with Beef Or Salmon pulling up – he was found to be suffering from a virus. Kicking King had turned the tables on Salmon at Punchestown in early December, but when Michael Hourigan's chestnut then scalped triple Gold Cup victor Best Mate at Leopardstown at Christmas, there were many who felt the Irish horse could go the whole way and win the big one. It wasn't to be, yet as Michael Hourigan says, look at what he has achieved in his career.

NAVAN

Set in 181 acres in the royal county of Meath, Navan boasts one of the most impressive courses in Ireland. An undulating oblong of one and a half miles round, it also has a six-furlong sprint track – and a top-notch 18-hole golf course within its grounds (free racing included for all members).

It remembers some great Irish horses both on the Flat and in jumping with a €70,000 Listed Salsabil race for fillies in April and a Listed Vintage Crop race in May. In November it remembers Fortria, For Auction (winner of the 1982 Champion Hurdle for local trainer Michael Cunningham), Monksfield and the horse who perhaps originally put Navan on the map: Troytown, the Aintree Grand National winner of 1920, who was trained nearby.

My own abiding Navan memory is that of Dawn Run's first chase on a wet autumn day in 1984. Ridden by a confident, smiling Tony Mullins, she jumped superbly and easily swept aside her lifelong rivals Buck House and Dark Ivy.

Navan has gone down the corporate route, and the popular direction of themed days for racegoers. Family day in May is just that, whether or not some of the attractions have much to do with racing, like clowns, face-painting and a mini funfair for the children, fortune teller, free pony rides, and Coke and ice cream. Summer meetings will incorporate barbecue and jazz evenings, and country and western evenings; Ladies Day in October is played to background music by the Navan Silver Band.

Navan, already one of the best courses in Ireland, is set to build new stables, a weigh-room complex and a children's play area. It is also constructing a new owners', trainers' and members' bar, affording a view of the paddock from its balcony, plus an extension to current bars and eating places.

* * *

Navan has always attracted local talent, none more so than Ireland's leading NH trainer, Noel Meade, who lives a few miles away. Noel was born and raised to be a farmer. No horses or racing in the family, yet the passion stirred in him as a schoolboy and never left. It brings good days and 'bloody awful' days. 'But,' says Noel, 'racing has become part of my life. And look what a tough time farmers have had.'

He adds, 'My father thought all people with thoroughbreds went broke, but to be fair to him he never stopped me.'

It was in 1968 that Noel Meade, aged 17, and a friend, neighbouring dairy farmer Michael Condra, paid 100 guineas to Buster Harty for a pin-fired horse in Ballsbridge sales, Dublin. This horse, Tu Va, was the start of his love affair with racing. Appropriately it is after him that his house is named.

Tu Va was a true fun horse who placed every time he ran and gave the 6 ft 1 in. Noel his only riding success, in an amateur riders' maiden hurdle at Wexford in the late 1960s. One Dermot Weld, champion amateur rider and now champion flat trainer, was second.

Noel Meade's house lies halfway down the smart avenue that leads to the stables and the old family home from where his brother, Ben, has continued with the farming. A line of schooling fences on an all-weather surface greet the visitor and everywhere there is a sense that the property is well maintained. It is up in the north of Co. Meath near a village called Castletown, almost equidistant from the towns of Navan, Ardee, Slane and Kells.

Two horses from his earliest training days still provide Noel Meade with his best memories: Pinch Hitter (a baseball term) and Steel Duke, who were both Galway Festival specialists. Pinch Hitter was owned by Finbar and Mairead Cahill, good friends of Noel's – 'always had great fun with them', he says – and Steel Duke, owned by another friend, Jim McKeown, and others.

'They are the horses that got me rolling and I still think the first Galway Hurdle [of two] with Pinch Hitter is my best racing memory. We celebrated all week; we hadn't expected big things. The owner, a retired solicitor, was a great character, genuine and down-to-earth.' Fun and friends are two words that

The lady sellers of fruit and chocolate are a familiar sight outside many Irish racecourses

feature frequently in Noel Meade's vocabulary.

The early days mostly involved flat horses: Sweet Mint, a filly who won at Royal Ascot, and in the late '90s, Sunshine Street, a colt who, in Noel's words, took him all over the world.

Owned by Pat Garvey, the American-bred colt finished second on his first five starts at Cork, Leopardstown and The

Noel Meade and Gillian O'Brien

Curragh, in two of those being beaten by a head and a short head. He then travelled to Epsom to run in the 1998 Epsom Derby where, starting at 150–1 and ridden by Johnny Murtagh, he finished a far-from-disgraced fourth, only two lengths behind the winner, High Rise.

'He went to every Group 1 dance that year,' Noel Meade recalls. 'He was fifth in the King George [to Daylami], third in the St Leger [to Nedawi] and fifth in the Breeders' Cup Turf. We also took him to Dubai, but he was injured there before the race.' Sunshine Street may only have won two races, but he certainly gave his connections a great deal of fun.

It was in the mid-1990s that Noel and

his long-time partner and assistant trainer Gillian O'Brien decided to concentrate on NH racing. 'It was the rise of Ballydoyle, the Aga Khan and the Arabs, paying such high prices at the sales that we couldn't compete at the top level, so we switched,' explains Noel.

'Jumping is tough, it is a much harder game; training flat horses is a doddle by comparison, they don't have so many injuries, don't have to have as much work, and they don't have to work so far. It is the injuries in jumping that are the heartbreakers.'

He cites Tiananmen Square as an example. He won the Champion Bumper in Punchestown, beating Montelado, and he won his first two hurdles, but then he was sidelined. He came back from injury and beat Dorans Pride and was second to Flakey Dove, but then injury again prevented him proving his true worth on the track.

'He was one hell of a horse,' remembers Noel.

Another was Johnny Setaside. The seven year old had already won or placed in 12 of his 18 races when he contested the Ericsson Chase (Grade 1) at Leopardstown on 28 December 1996 for his owners, John O'Meara, Johnny Farrell and Mark Jackson. The horse had won on his first hurdle attempt in November 1994 and again on his first chase a year later; he was quickly moving up the chasing tree. His wins included the Drinmore Novices Chase (Grade 1) at Fairyhouse in December 1995, a Grade 3 at Punchestown the following February and a Grade 3 chase at Fairyhouse in November 1996. It was little wonder that the bay by Remainder Man went off favourite for the Ericsson a month later.

Jumping superbly throughout the three miles and always 'up with the pace', Johnny Setaside ran out a convincing three-length winner of the race that has been won since by the likes of Beef Or Salmon and Best Mate. But sadly as Johnny Setaside was returning to the unsaddling enclosure, he suffered a heart attack and dropped down dead.

Racing, and especially steeplechasing, is a great leveller.

Far from his days of training one or two horses, Noel can now accommodate up to a hundred, of which maybe a dozen will be for the Flat and for which he has a multinational staff. Roughly 50 per cent are Irish, such as James Wilkinson – 'a great help' – and the rest are Czech, Polish, Lithuanian, Russian and Argentinian. Libu, a Czech girl, is one of his stars, and Antonio, from Argentina, is another.

'But,' says Noel, 'I don't know how I could go on without my head lad, Paul Cullen, who has been with me right since I started, and his number two, Damian McGillick, as well as Peter Kavanagh, my main work rider over the last ten years, since he gave up being jockey to Paddy Mullins.'

Jockey Paul Carberry is a crucial part of the whole set-up, but Noel reserves the biggest praise of all for his partner Gillian, daughter of Phonsie O'Brien, niece of Vincent. 'She is my right hand and has been for the 20 years we've been together.'

Gillian rode in one point-to-point in the United States and took over the training from her father when he retired, until she moved to Meath. She still rides out in Noel's string. Growing up with Phonsie was always great fun, she says. 'He was, and still is, a great lover of life; the life and soul of any party.'

Noel has been leading NH trainer in Ireland seven times (judged on the number of wins) and champion trainer five times (on prize money won; Willie Mullins has beaten him in the other two). Sausalito Bay's win in the Supreme Novices Hurdle over Best Mate at the Cheltenham Festival in 2000 and The Bunny Boiler's victory in the 2002 Irish Grand National for the Usual Suspects syndicate remain Noel's biggest wins. They gave him, in his words, 'a special buzz'. The consistent Harbour Pilot has twice been third in the Cheltenham Gold Cup, but at the time of writing is sidelined, whereas Harchibald was one of the top-seven priced Irish horses for the 2005 Smurfit Champion Hurdle. In a memorable race Harchibald went down by only a neck to reigning champion Hardy Eustace, with Brave Inca another neck away in third. It was a controversial race in that Paul Carberry sat as still as he could on Harchibald until the last moment, but when he applied the pressure there was nothing left in the tank.

Mannix Dowdall, 60 years
a groundsman at Navan

Brave Inca, who was hard-ridden up the final hill, equally couldn't quite peg back the winner.

'It does bring so much pressure,' Noel confesses, 'I sometimes wonder if I would be better off small again.'

But somehow one doubts it.

In fact, it is Harchibald's owner, Des Sharkey, and the High Street Syndicate, made up of Dublin businessmen, that has enabled Noel to acquire more expensive horses and, with them, the bigger opportunities. 'From the start I felt Harchibald was good and as a three year old even said I thought he was a Champion Hurdler in the making, but then he became disappointing, until a wind operation put him right again.

'He's a lovely horse and character. We bought him at the Arc sale in France, where he had won a few races in the south-west for a small trainer.'

Noel Meade is highly regarded and respected not only as a trainer and a person but also as a director of Navan racecourse, in which role he can advise on the framing of races and various other matters from a participant's point of view. But he says the biggest credit for the rise in the fortunes of Navan should go to its indefatigable chairman, William Flood, a stud owner from Trim.

'He not only works tirelessly but also bull-headedly,' says Noel. 'He'll put his head in where other people wouldn't put a toe; he wouldn't accept a "go away and forget about it" answer. Now he's senior NH steward. There's no doubt that Navan wouldn't be where it is today without William.'

* * *

As Noel Meade praises William Flood, so Mannix Dowdall, Navan groundsman for 60 years, salutes both men. It was not so much a case of finding a job for life for Mannix as of the job finding him.

For sixty-three years Mannix was groundsman at Navan racecourse until eventually, at four score years, he was persuaded to retire. But not even that can keep him away on race days; you'll find him helping down at the start, his alert 84-

year-old eyes ever watchful for whatever might be needed.

It was when his father, who was also Navan groundsman, was off work with an injury that schoolboy Mannix used to collect his father's wages for him on a Friday evening. Before long, unofficially, he was doing his father's work and being paid for it. When his father returned to work, Mannix continued working too.

'Well, no one ever asked me not to come,' he explains. He stayed for more than 60 years, and for his 80th birthday a race was named after him at the January meeting. He leans on the balcony of the smart new restaurant and clubhouse (for racing and golfing members alike) and looks out on the stretching view of the Co. Meath countryside, to the Tara Mines, the Mullagh Hill at Oldcastle, three little hills in Westmeath known as the Ben of Fore, and on into Co. Cavan. He loves this stretch of land, and he knows every blade of grass, every clod of earth on the track. Beyond it lies the 2,000 acres that was once part of the Fitzherbert Estate in Gibbstown, famous for being Troytown's birthplace and training grounds.

It was in about 1920 that some local farmers got together to start a racecourse. There were no tractors, and the land that is now the smooth, one-and-a-half-mile-round racecourse, encasing a billiard-green, sought-after golf course, was knocked into basic shape by men pushing wheelbarrows, guiding horses and carts, and manually removing big banks by hand, ready for the opening in 1921 (the year Mannix Dowdall was born). Mannix's father, Phil, told him that the embryo committee became heavily in debt a few short years later, to the mighty sum in those days of £13,000, and the bank closed on them. But the intrepid committee managed to buy it back and clear the debt, then ran the course with aplomb until the Racing Board took it over in the 1980s, by which time most of the original shareholders were dead.

'We now have a great committee here,' Mannix says, 'headed by William Flood, with Noel Meade – we couldn't have a better man – and an excellent manager in Richard Lyttle, who thinks of everyone. I love keeping in touch with the girls in the office and helping down at the start on race days.'

Mannix recalls his daily work, mowing, harrowing and rolling, using a pony and cart in the early days. 'No walkie-talkies then, let alone mobile phones,' he says.

'We used to make the timber frames for the fences from oak planks; it was a big job. And then we'd collect the birch from Fletcherstown bog. Later it used to be delivered by lorry. The fences are measured now; they used to be tougher and there wasn't so much emphasis on safety. I can remember when helmets weren't worn at all, but I'm all for the extra safety measures, like plastic rails – it used to be stock fence.

'Until the foot-and-mouth epidemic of 1967 the centre of the course had been used for grazing stock, but after that it all became tillage.

'I remember an air display here in 1936. There were seven planes and it cost 2s 6d for a flight, but I didn't have enough money so I didn't go up. I've only been to England twice in my life; most of my schoolpals emigrated or joined the war and never came back.

'I remember owners like Colonel Hill Dillon and trainers like Tom Dreaper, Dan

Jack High, winner of the Troytown Chase 2004 for owner Brenda Ross, trainer Ted Walsh and rider Gary Cotter

Moore, Des McDonogh, Charlie McCartin. There were very few complaints about the course.'

Among the horses he remembers running at Navan are Prince Regent, Dawn Run, Monksfield, L'Escargot and, more recently, Danoli. And he remembers a certain day in January 1962 when the three-mile chase was won by Tom Dreaper's Last Link; his Ben Stack was expected to win the bumper, but didn't. And his mare Kerforo, winner of her previous three races and who was to go on and win her next three, was favourite for the novice hurdle in which another of Dreaper's was making his hurdling debut, having finished third and fourth in bumpers without troubling the winner in either. It was three miles of deep mud and at the finish it was the 20–1 outsider who cruised by Kerforo on a tight rein to score the first of his twenty-seven wins.

Arkle had arrived.

* * *

Another Dreaper horse particularly remembered at Navan is Fortria, after whom a chase is run each November. One of Jim Dreaper's earliest memories of his father's yard was as a nine-year-old boy when a padded straw ring was made on which Fortria was to have a hobday operation to correct a wind defect. Bred locally by Alec Craigie, of another enduring Co. Meath farming and hunting family, Fortria was a lovely stamp of horse. By the French stallion Fortina, who himself won the 1947 Cheltenham Gold Cup as a full horse, Fortria was out of a mare that Tom had previously trained to win a few races for Alec. Fortria won 20 races, 18 of them over fences. Tom Dreaper had also trained his dam, Senria, in the 1940s, to win a few races.

Fortria's wins included the Cotswold Chase at the Cheltenham Festival and the Two Mile (now Queen Mother) Champion Chase, and the Mackeson at what is now the Open meeting of Cheltenham in November. In a great weight-carrying performance, he also won the 1961 Irish Grand National carrying 12 st.

Monksfield, the tough dual Champion Hurdler trained not far from Navan by Des McDonogh, is also remembered at Navan with a novice hurdle run in his name in November on the same day as the Troytown Chase.

If ever there were a horse that epitomised the 'old-fashioned chaser', it was Troytown. Bred at the Co. Meath home of his owner, Major Thomas Collins-Gerrard, not far from Navan, he was a powerhouse of a horse: big, bold, a flamboyant jumper and strong with it; so strong that he tested the ability of even the best jockeys to hold him. In his first season racing as a six year old, he won the Grand Steeplechase de Paris (the French Grand National) at Auteuil, and the next year he took his chance at Aintree where Poethlyn was bidding for a hat-trick. But as that horse fell at the first, Troytown set off to make every post a winning post and, in driving rain that made the reins too slippery for his jockey, the great Jack Anthony, to grip, he looked like doing so. But a monumental blunder at the last open ditch left a hole in the fence that would have seen most perpetrators on the ground; it handed the lead to The Bore and Troytown's chance looked gone. But he was not a horse to give up that easily. He jumped past his rival at the last and powered his way up that infamous long run-in for a victory that made him admired and popular on both sides of the Irish Sea. It was incredibly sad that he lost his life a few short months later when he broke a leg back at Auteuil, the same course at which Dawn Run lost her life not long after her epic Cheltenham Gold Cup win some six decades later.

The current Navan management found a unique painted and framed commemoration of Troytown's Grand National victory tucked away in a downstairs office and had it restored. The calligraphy used to make it contains 25 colours per square inch, a feat that is estimated would take some 18 months to reproduce by hand. It now hangs in the clubroom. It is fitting that Troytown is remembered at Navan.

DECEMBER

LIMERICK

The stunning new track at Greenmount Park, Patrickswell, near Limerick, was the result of the canny foresight of one man, Hugh McMahon, and then of an unusually on-song committee. Add to that the professional and youthful touch of manager Angus Houston and you have a recipe for success.

That success, says Angus Houston, came about through the meeting of many minds at numerous meetings. 'They all had different ideas about where to put the stands or site the winning post or place the fences and so on, but they all gelled and ended up with nothing flawed.'

It was Hugh McMahon who came up with the original idea and persuaded the committee to buy the 280-acre site a few miles out of Limerick city in 1996.

Limerick, or rather Greenmount Park, the classy title Lord Harrington suggested, whose Greenmount Stud lent its name to the brand image, deserves all the accolades heaped on it since its opening in October 2001. It is a far cry from its run-down city predecessor, which had eight 'mediocre to poor' race days, and some of those would be lost to the weather. The 120-year-old course was looking distinctly aged by that time. In Angus Houston, the committee came up with an inspired choice. A Scottish graduate of the catering industry, his only previous connection with racing was through his work for Letherby and

Greenmount Park: view of Limerick racecourse from the stand

Christopher, the eponymous caterers at many British racecourses.

Angus brought a business brain and marketing strategy to the job, and then more: like many other Irish racecourses, Limerick derives much of its income from renting out its gallops to trainers on non-race days (including the Irish practice of running schooling bumpers giving young horses unofficial racing experience). A number of trainers and riders began to complain about the all-weather track. Angus was not in a position to understand the veracity or not of this, so he took riding lessons and before long he was riding daily on the gallops himself. That way he was able to interact with other users and to

differentiate between wool-pulling and genuine grievances.

There was a nice offshoot to this for Angus, who, with his newly acquired riding skill, took up polo; he claims to have the 'best pony there is' in the failed hurdler Donn Or by Rock Hopper. 'I like the fast, competitive team spirit of polo,' he says.

The first impression of Greenmount Park is one of expanse: the track is set in a large oval and a lake has been formed in the interior. The stands and car parks are on a natural grandstand overlooking the whole course, affording superb viewing of the racing, and Co. Limerick seems to stretch endlessly around. The site is so roomy that it boasts no less than five parallel tracks and still has space for more: the chase course takes up the wide outside, the boundary fence guiding horses up and over four inviting, gently uphill fences on the far side, before taking another on the right-hand turn at the top of the hill. It has a bumper course of its own (instead of having to remove the hurdles for the end-of-card bumper, as at most courses). The hurdle track comes next and on its inside is the all-weather schooling gallop which runners use on race days to canter down to the start (no kick-back, I noticed), and finally on the inside is the flat track. There is no five-furlong straight, but the course nevertheless deserves its Grade 1 status.

As I walked round during the Christmas meeting, the ground was desperately heavy, but at every fence there was a group of workmen not only replacing divots but, where necessary, filling them in with sand from a pile by each fence, complete with bucket and spade. 'It was worse earlier in the week,' one of them told me. 'It's dried a bit today.'

'Not so,' said the clerk of the course, Peter McGouran, when I bumped into him later on, 'but fresh ground is used each day.'

Some of Limerick's legendary heroes are well remembered here. On the human side, the spacious, well-designed grandstand is named after the new course's brainchild, Hugh McMahon. Within it is the Dorans Pride bar named after Michael Hourigan's stalwart and very popular chaser (see Ballinrobe). On the third day of its Christmas festival, Dorans Pride has his own race named after him too.

Imperial Call (see Roscommon), Irish winner of the Cheltenham Gold Cup in 1996, has his own bar in the stand at Limerick.

The great Martin Molony is usually on hand each summer to present the trophy to the winner of the flat race named after him – apart from being one of the best steeplechase jockeys of his generation, Martin Molony was also ace on the Flat, having won the 1950 Irish 1,000 Guineas on a horse called Princess Trudy and the 1951 Irish 2,000 Guineas on a horse called Signal Box.

Dorans Pride bar

Another feature of the summer is the revived annual Jockeys Challenge between the UK and Ireland. Until being resurrected in 2003, it had not been held since 1985. The series of four hurdle races takes place in early July. Ireland won the first two renewals then made it a clean sweep three out of three for the home side in 2005.

Another specialist Limerick racehorse, the mare Shannon Spray, got her own race in March 2005. Shannon Spray was a prolific winner for local trainer Austin Leahy. Owned by Father Jack Fitzgerald, she won her first five hurdle races, all of them at Limerick. A chestnut mare born in 1981 by Le Bavard out of a Menelek mare, she won nine, was second five times and

Hurdling at Limerick

king, when his Good Step, owned by J.P. McManus runs out a comfortable winner. But back at the last fence Was I Right falls heavily and lies unmoving on top of his jockey, Roger Quinlan, who is trapped under him, as more horses approach the fence. Seconds seem like minutes in such circumstances and by the time the horse is manually rolled over, and the jockey hauled out from under him, enough time has gone by for the now-riveted crowd to applaud from the grandstand as Roger walks away, with barely a limp.

It was the end of four festive days and for those so inclined, there was a free bus service to two of Limerick city's favourite bars . . .

* * *

third twice from twenty NH runs, a wonderful record.

* * *

It is easy, on my Christmas visit, to see why the new Limerick is proving so popular. Pearly Jack is also popular, carrying top weight and running for the second time in the week to justify favouritism in the two-mile six-furlong chase ridden by 7 lb-claimer M.J. O'Connor for restricted trainer D.E. Fitzgerald. It is another claimer, Michael Darcy, whose 5 lb off Paddy's Girl helps him get up on long-time leader Vitellius in the closest finish of the day.

Most dramatic, though, came as Enda Bolger showed why he is hunter chase

The new track has given Limerick the opportunity to retrench, move up and on. With its re-brand Grade 1 hat on, Limerick is expanding from 17 to 20 race days a year. Some of its biggest attendances are at the summer-evening flat meetings, with thousands flocking in from the nearby city. There is so much space that there is never a scrum, yet it somehow retains a friendly atmosphere. 'We also have thousands of non-racing packages,' Angus Houston says. 'We have got to expand the market; we're in the leisure and entertainment business.'

Non-racing occasions include the well-established Limerick County Show each

182

August, the Irish Truckfest, a circus, the Irish Motorbike Festival and even the Munster Bridal Exhibition. Banquets can cater for up to 2,000 seated diners, and the amount of space available, both indoors and out, makes it an ideal venue for music concerts and festivals.

Talking of music, most of the summer meetings feature post-race bands, and it is not unusual to see racegoers dancing the night away.

Patrickswell is home not only to Greenmount Park/Limerick racecourse, but also to the Hourigan family and their well-run and thriving training stable. Even when trainer Michael Hourigan was away saddling at Leopardstown over the Christmas meeting, the name Hourigan was still much in evidence at their local track. Son Michael was busy taking professional photographs, while daughter Kay was coerced in front of the paddock microphone to tell racegoers how Beef Or Salmon, the stable star, was 24 hours after his memorable scalping of triple Cheltenham Gold Cup champion Best Mate, no less. 'He's been out in the field for two or three hours, messin',' she told his fans.

* * *

Cat and mouse. Grandmother's footsteps. Cloak and dagger.

Games. Serious stuff.

The gates are locked. Horses have to be

Beef or Salmon with his devoted lass, Kay Hourigan

Trainer Michael Hourigan with jockey Ruby Walsh

183

jumped in and out over stone walls off the road to reach their (illicit) training grounds. They come from various back gardens in the village of Rathkeale, Co. Limerick, and from behind the pub where the trainer lives. He has no land of his own, not even an acre. He has to duck and dive, in and out of other people's land to exercise his horses – always respects it, though, going in single file around the edges.

One day a landowner stops him. 'Whose got the licence in this village, you or me?'

'Well, I have,' the trainer replies.

'Then use your own land.'

With that, he locks all four gates. Then he takes to leaving one unlocked, on a rota basis. It was a tacit, unspoken arrangement, acknowledgement even, that the young trainer was trying to earn a living.

Son of a 6 ft 2 in. cattle dealer and publican, the 5 ft 4 in. Michael Hourigan took to hanging around the local stables rather than going to school. Johnny Fellenn, who kept show horses, took the lad to the major shows all over the country and taught him to ride.

'I was a disaster at school and hardly ever went,' Michael admits, 'so eventually I was made to go to Rockwell College for a year to learn to read and write. I left in June 1962 [at the age of 14] and in August I started as an apprentice to Charlie Weld, Dermot's father, on The Curragh.

'They were the best days of my life, hard work but fabulous and always hoping for a ride. Mrs Weld [Gita] was absolutely fantastic.'

After his five-year apprenticeship, which produced nine winners, Michael moved to Jimmy O'Connell in Blanchardstown, Dublin, and then, with rising weight, changed over to the jumping game with Commander Crawford (father of the equine artist Susan) just outside Edinburgh. 'I bluffed my way into the job. I'd never schooled a racehorse and hunting as a kid was very different.'

Two weeks later, Michael was put up on a mare in a twenty-three-runner novice chase at Newcastle. Only three finished, but Michael was second. 'I thought I was a jockey,' he says, 'then she ran again the following Saturday and was killed, broke her back.'

Michael learnt about the downside early in his racing life. He rode one chase and three hurdle winners, 'but I wasn't cut out for it,' he says.

A spell with Lord Petersham at Patrickswell, Limerick, ended in a sacking and so in 1973, at the age of 25 (the same year he married Anne Wall), Michael took out a licence and trained between one and three, and back to one horse at any time, and earned a few bob by driving a horsebox. After six years of this he looked across at the bakery one New Year's Eve and vowed that if things didn't pick up soon, he would drive the baker's van, no other choice.

Shortly afterwards he met an old friend, Robert Hawkins, at the sales, and transported some purchases home for him. Robert Hawkins then offered him one of them to train.

The horse, Ramrajya, had bowed tendons, indicating past strains on both front legs, but he was set to alter Michael's life.

It was 2.10 p.m. on 17 March, St Patrick's Day, 1979, that Ramrajya, ridden by Jackie Cullen, father of current jockey John, came home the 20–1 winner for Michael's first success as a trainer. It was at the old Limerick Greenpark racecourse, a time and place and moment that are indelibly ingrained in Michael's conscience.

'I will never forget it as long as I live,' says Michael, 'there is no other feeling like it, the greatest thrill.'

All wins are great, but there is only ever one first win, and Michael happily savours the moment, reliving that tingling sensation. Two others rate up there with that: Tropical Lake, who gave him his first win in England, in the Glenlivet Hurdle at Aintree, and his first Cheltenham Festival winner with Dorans Pride in the Stayers' Hurdle. 'I shall never forget the commentator saying, "And look at Dorans Pride on the outside, he's cantering."' That tingle factor again.

But that sort of occasion was still well in the future. Ramrajya set the ball dribbling rather than rolling; Michael trained five

winners that season and twelve the following year in 1980. He increased to 22 horses, still dotted all over the village in various backyards and still without a gallop. Eventually he was able to rent an old stud with 36 stables and a cottage, but with the cost in rent it was difficult to make ends meet. The stubble that the horses worked on cut their heels and a good gallop was badly needed.

Enter a block of 67 acres for sale with a dilapidated cottage and cow byre at Lisaleen, Patrickswell. Today an acre of that is covered in concrete and buildings, 105 stables (rubble floors covered in rubber matting plus shavings) with perky horses' heads looking out, a huge indoor swimming pool, two uphill all-weather five-furlong gallops, one of sand, the other woodchip, a line of schooling fences, stud-railed paddocks, two indoor schools, 'hotels' for the lads, a room for infrared lamp treatment for the horses – and a fine, large family house.

Back then it was a matter of how to pay for the bare land, let alone build anything on it. Throughout his barely viable days Michael Hourigan had a good friend in his bank manager, Jerry O'Connell, who remains a personal friend today, along with his wife, Marjie. On the day that the sale price of £110,000 was agreed, 5 May 1985, and an £11,000 deposit paid, the local vendor volunteered to allow Michael to move his horses there that night. Two days later, Michael thought to himself,

'Where on earth am I going to get £100,000 from?'

'If I hadn't already moved the horses, I do believe I would have pulled out there and then, and forfeited the deposit,' he says.

That October, Michael and Anne Hourigan, their family increasing, crammed into the old two-up, two-down cottage. The first thing to do was put in a £90,000 all-weather gallop. It went wrong. Badly. The matter went to court. Michael lost the case.

Once again Jerry O'Connell came to the rescue 'and we got through somehow'. It was an inauspicious start to Lisaleen, but 'Jerry was my backbone'.

A few winners started appearing. Michael does not bet, but he made some money by selling one or two horses for a profit – one of them, Lisaleen Prince, for £50,000 in about 1989. A great believer in the tonic of the sea, an equine swimming pool was installed at a cost of £54,000. The sea is still used, too; horses regularly being boxed up to visit Beale beach or the banks of the River Shannon, not only for the sea water, but also the change of scene.

By 1995, with their fifth child on the way, the Hourigans finally set about building a fair-sized home for themselves. The block-work for it had reached about 5 ft high when a twenty-acre parcel of land next door came up for sale. The house building was suspended. The land was bought. The patient Anne continued to cope with the little cottage.

Racing for the Hourigans is a family affair: two of the children, Paul and Laura, have won races on Beef Or Salmon; Kay nurtures Beef Or Salmon with her whole being and also runs the yard; Laura, who drives the lorry and helps with the horses, has won over hurdles, in point-to-points and ten bumpers; Michael junior is himself a trainer; Paul, who rode a number of winners as a professional, now works in property for Alfred Buller of Scarvagh House and Sandley Studs; and Mark, whose 11th birthday was on Cheltenham Gold Cup day 2005, is still at school.

By the time the large house was finally built some of the older children were moving away, but any lunchtime, with Anne's homemade soup and cake on the table, there is still a big family gathered in the kitchen.

Michael has won three Kerry Nationals, a Galway Plate and a Powers Gold Cup, but not an Irish National – yet. His main ambition, though, is 'to be like Paddy Mullins'.

'I have so much admiration for him and I never thought he would retire. He was the quiet man of racing; he doesn't say much, but is a gentleman. No matter what success he had, he was always still Paddy Mullins and never changed. I hope I will always be just Michael Hourigan.'

The state of Irish racing, he says, is 'very, very healthy'.

'Everyone wants to own a racehorse, and they should be able to. I think Horse

Racing Ireland is wrong to want to reduce the number of runners by weeding out the bottom end; back in the 1980s we had only three or four runners per race in the summer, and we don't want that to happen again. We should let the horses run: bad will beat worse and extra days for these horses could be held inside current courses, there is plenty of land; top of the ground [firm going] should be allowed, too, rather than watering, to cater for horses that do best on firm.'

Michael Hourigan loves all three Kerry tracks – Killarney, Listowel and Tralee – and he also loves point-to-pointing. He has won races on every course in Ireland (and likes them all) and at every festival. He has also started a number of 'boys' in their careers as jockeys, including Adrian Maguire (who trained his first winner in spring 2005), Robbie Supple, David Casey and Johnny Kavanagh.

'The bollickings came free; it was a way of getting things through to them, giving them a chance. I have some very good kids in the yard. There'll be one who is temperamental and another who just keeps smiling.

Who needs a jockey?

'The horses have been good to me,' Michael adds.

And in a horse called Moss Bank, a point-to-point winner in 2005, he believes he has the horse that will one day fill Beef Or Salmon's shoes.

Looking at the eighty-five contented horses and the acres of facilities, Michael Hourigan has come a long way from one horse in the backyard of a pub. But he is still the same Michael Hourigan.

CORK

It was famously in Co. Cork that the supposed first steeplechase took place, over a five-mile tract of land between the churches of Buttevant and Doneraile in 1752. It is also the county from which Captain Becher hailed, after whom the famous brook is named at Aintree – he was decanted into the brook after his horse, Conrad, fell there during the first running of the Grand National in 1839.

More local races like the Buttevant to Doneraile ones proliferated through the eighteenth century, often matches between two hunters, usually with a distant church steeple to aim for. Thus was 'steeple chasing' born, or the practice of racing from 'point to point'. Down the generations since, point-to-pointing has become the amateur version, or nursery ground, of steeplechasing.

Cork is Ireland's largest county and maintains its tradition of hunting, from which the twin sports of steeplechasing and point-to-pointing stem. Mallow is a thriving town on the River Blackwater and by 1777 the embryonic sport, by now with some organisation and rules, held six consecutive days of racing in the area, 'all to be run according to the King's Plate articles'.

Racing was held at Cork Park until 1917, but when that ceased, the county was left without a racecourse, an omission that did not last long thanks to the determination of Lieutenant Colonel F.F. MacCabe, who founded and ran the track at Mallow in 1924. Racing has taken place there ever since, apart from a spell in the 1990s when the track underwent a €9 million refurbishment and drainage scheme. When it reopened in 1997, it was also re-christened Cork racecourse to take account of the whole county and its interest in racing.

Bound by the River Blackwater on two sides, Cork racecourse is absolutely flat. This, and its proximity to the river, have almost inevitably led to flooding over the years, although much has been done to alleviate it, and Cork holds fixtures throughout the year. Although it can, on occasion, still lose a meeting to floods, it probably means it's a safe bet that it will never be developed for housing – unless they are built on stilts! The course drains very quickly and will be raceable within a few days of being flooded. It is an attractive, oblong course of one and a half miles, which suits an out-and-out galloper; the chase course has three fences down each long side, both including an open ditch, and a 'cross' fence at both ends. When the horses turn for home, they still have a long way and three fences to cover. The view of the whole course from the excellent new stand is outstanding.

On the Flat it boasts a six-furlong straight. At Easter it holds a three-day festival and in December it stages its principal race of the year, the Hilly Way Chase.

Hilly Way twice won the Two Mile Champion Chase at the Cheltenham NH Festival – in 1978 ridden by Tommy Carmody and in 1979 by Ted Walsh, for owner J. Sweeney and trainer Peter McCreery, the year before that race became the 'Queen Mother'.

My visit at Easter 2005 sees a glorious spring day and a good mixed card of two flat, two hurdles and two steeplechases, plus a bumper. The feature is the three-mile Imperial Call Chase, won by GVA Ireland, the youngest horse in the race, trained by Francis Flood and ridden by Robbie Power. The combination runs on too strongly for the favourite, Joueur D'Estruval, trained by Willie Mullins and ridden by Ruby Walsh for owner Mrs Violet O'Leary, owner of the now retired Florida Pearl.

There is a sentimental result to the two-and-a-half-mile handicap chase, producing a first ever win on his 22nd attempt for the grey Harry In A Hurry. The race pans out more like a novice chase, with several of the runners falling, but that doesn't detract from Harry, who I last saw attempting the massive marathon that is the Velka Pardubice, the Czech Grand National, the previous October. A few of the fences on that twisting course make even Aintree look small, and Harry had jumped the biggest two, the infamous Taxis and the even bigger double-spread hedge, but then was interfered with and fell heavily at the tenth. He lay on the

Harry In A Hurry breaks his maiden tag in Cork

ground for a few minutes, and it was a relief to see him get up. He had to be a good jumper to be considered for such a race, but was probably deemed to have a 'touch of the slows', although he had once finished second to Rathgar Beau in a ten-runner chase at Limerick back in December 2002 and was runner-up again at Gowran Park in January 2004 in an eighteen-runner handicap chase. A second of 16 at Thurles in February 2005 set him right for this race in Cork and it is a real pleasure to see him win, in the hands of 3 lb-claimer Tom Ryan, who ended the season leading conditional rider.

The tradition of farming and keeping one or two horses to race is steeped in Irish folklore, more so in Co. Cork than

Action at Cork races (Mallow)

greatest NH mare of all time. Her name was Dawn Run.

At that time Patrick Mangan had already bred the 1956 Champion Hurdle winner, Doorknocker, and the evergreen Waterloo Boy, who gave lots of success during the 1980s to his four-strong team of farmer owners in England.

At the time of Dawn Run's birth, one of Patrick Mangan's seven sons, Jimmy 'J.J.' Mangan, was an aspiring point-to-point rider. Like his father, Jimmy went on to breed, deal and train a few, notably future Grand National-winner Bindaree, which he bought as a yearling and sold as a three year old. He also bred Amble Speedy, who was to come within a short head of winning the 1997 Irish Grand National, trained by Arthur Moore. But since the turn of the century, into the new millennium, there has been another famous name added to the Mangan household.

As I drove into the village in November 2003, the sign for Conna was heralded with 'Home of 2003 Grand National Winner Monty's Pass'. It is the custom of the organisers of Aintree to launch their next Grand National meeting at the stables of the previous winner, and for the assembled friends and press to view the stable's inmates before enjoying lunch (salmon from the nearby River Blackwater is on this particular menu) and speeches outlining the sponsors' and organisers' plans for the next national.

anywhere else. Some will train, some will breed or take in boarders, perhaps a mare to foal or a youngster to break, others will deal, but most will do all of these things. The Mangan household in Conna, near Mallow, is typical and has been for generations.

* * *

It was as twilight fell on 27 April 1978 that Patrick Mangan quietly watched a visiting mare safely give birth to a filly foal. She had a white star and long bay ears. It had been an easy foaling and so just two days later mother and foal returned to their owner near Rathcormack. It would have been an easily forgettable two days but for one thing: the filly foal was to become the

It is an occasion not only to see the latest winner as well as young horses coming on, but also to glimpse the future Mangan generation, for the diminutive Paddy Mangan, Jimmy and Mary's son, is not only leading round Monty's Pass, but is also already a leading pony racer with many wins under his belt.

This branch of racing is almost exclusive to Ireland, though an attempt was made to start it in Great Britain under Jockey Club and Pony Club auspices in the summer of 2004. It has been the nursery school of many of Ireland's top jockeys, where they have learnt the art of jockeyship round the fields or beaches. Pony racing culminates with the Dingle Derby in Kerry each August.

At the Mangans' in Conna on Grand National launch day, only four of the thirteen horses are named, headed, of course, by Monty's Pass, along with Sigma Dotcom, See More Bills and Suberlette.

Among the youngsters is a five-year-old mare by Anshan from the same family as Arkle, a four-year-old full brother to Silver Birch, as well as Rosalier, Beneficial and Oscar four year olds, and some nice three year olds.

'Most of the horses here are young NH horses starting out on their careers,' Jimmy explains. 'Monty is one that was left with us after he won his point-to-points and hunter chase.'

Does he rue selling on those that turn out stars? Not a bit. 'I like to see them win

The diminutive Paddy Mangan, already winning pony races, here parading Grand National-winner Monty's Pass

when they leave the yard and give people fun,' he says.

But it was still sweet to see a little stable win the mighty Aintree Grand National, beating the 'big boys' in the process.

Monty's Pass ran another cracker in the 2004 Grand National, running on to be fourth behind fellow Irish-bred Amberleigh House trained by Ginger 'Red Rum' McCain. Monty's Pass is out of a mare by dual Champion Hurdler Monksfield and was bred by G. Slattery.

Monty had already shown his aptitude for the Aintree fences and for staying

races prior to his Aintree National win, having finished second of 28 in the Topham Chase. He also won the Kerry National in Listowel and placed in the Galway Plate.

It was, appropriately, at Cork that he won his first race under NH Rules, a hunter chase, and from six runs on the Mallow track he has only once been unplaced. Probably the most spectacular win there was on his return from his summer holiday after winning the Grand National. A charity flat race, he was ridden by Jimmy's wife, Mary, and carried 12 st. 6 lb, much of it made up in deadweight.

It remains the only flat race Monty's Pass has ever run in, though like many other Irish trainers, Jimmy Mangan runs him over hurdles quite regularly and has preceded his National runs with hurdle races. In the 2005 Grand National Monty's Pass was unable to threaten the leaders, but he still finished the course.

DUNDALK

Arkle wouldn't recognise it. But then more than two score years have passed since 'Himself' won a hurdle in October 1963 at what can now be dubbed 'old Dundalk'. It was the Wee Handicap Hurdle worth £163 and the five-year-old Arkle carried 11 st. 13 lb to victory over the sharp two miles and one furlong, pricking his majestic ears as he passed the packed stand. That was the day when his jockey, the late Pat Taaffe, first discovered the acceleration Arkle possessed.

Today the old stand has gone. A state-of-the-art glass-fronted pavilion offering 180-degree views has replaced it. A 550-yard silica-sand greyhound track, the biggest in Europe, sits beyond the old winning post. It represents the laid egg, with the nest that will surround it yet to be built. At the time of writing, part of the old grass course and winning stretch can still be picked out, but by 2006 it should be covered in the most up-to-date surface.

All-weather racing is about to arrive in Ireland. There will be a minimum of twenty-five meetings per year of eight races a time; two hundred new races per annum over any distance from five furlongs upwards. Not just for the bottom end of racing, either, for on each of its five Sunday meetings there will be a Listed race included. It should ease the balloting situation, possibly among hurdlers too, because some flat horses that were frequently being balloted out were being directed to hurdles instead. At one time Horse Racing Ireland had wanted the all-weather track to include hurdle races, but this plan has now been dropped on safety grounds. The new course will also be able to accommodate other flat fixtures transferred to them should a turf course be waterlogged.

Dundalk lies on the main road between Dublin and Belfast, halfway between these two cities. Ancient and modern meet here: there is the old port, the 300-year-old brewing and linen trades and the masses of recent retail outlets and new housing; the town is buzzing. Of the five million people in the island, nearly three million of them live within one and a half hours of Dundalk. And in early 2006 the Dundalk bypass is due to open, just 200 yards from the stadium. It is a fine example of location, location, location.

This exciting venture in Irish racing history is the result of the coming together of Dundalk's separate greyhound and horse-racing fraternities. Jim Martin, who became chief executive of the new joint venture in 2003, explains, 'Both venues were in the same position of being run-down and lacking in modern facilities.'

At the time, Jim, an accountant who was also a director of the greyhound stadium (as were his father and grandfather), wrote a module to redesign a greyhound track as part of a Master's course he was doing in business administration. 'That led me to think it

The state-of-the-art new stand at Dundalk for greyhound racing – it will be doubled in size when horse racing recommences

would be logical for the two businesses to come together. We began talks in 1996 and two years later agreed to combine and proceed.'

The old racecourse closed down in 2000 and, after some hold-ups, reconstruction started in 2002. Only the lovely old stable block remains. Dating from 1872, it originally housed a cavalry garrison and will be retained in some capacity, greeting the visitors as they drive in. The old greyhound stadium was sold off, as were a few acres of the racecourse – that land is already covered in new housing. But the view to the Carlingford Hills, and the snow-capped Mountains of Mourne peeking above and beyond them, remain unimpeded.

It was in November 2004 that Horse

Racing Ireland finally approved Dundalk's all-weather application, subject to the company coming up with €8 million (on top of the €11.5 million already spent) along with HRI's promise of €10 million. This will include doubling the size of the award-winning pavilion, creating the 10-furlong oval track, providing floodlights throughout and building 131 stables. One of the problems that had been overcome was by designing two chutes on the new course so that no start would be near a bend. Jim Martin also managed to reduce costs to levels acceptable to HRI.

It is hoped that there may be 2,000 customers on a Friday and 4,000 on the Sunday afternoons. The greyhound meetings average 1,000 on a Saturday when the Tote takes more than an average midweek horse-racing meeting.

When racing reopens at Dundalk, the venue will have the huge advantage of already being up and running as a greyhound track, complete with full-time staff. The new stadium was opened for greyhound racing in November 2003, when 3,000 people flocked through the turnstiles, a great reward for all the planning and effort that had gone into it.

Three evenings a week, Thursday to Saturday, that's one hundred and fifty days per year, hundreds of people come to watch the greyhound racing, to enjoy a bet, a meal, the company and the ambience. Well appointed throughout, the pavilion is fully carpeted with a specially commissioned greyhound and racehorse motif design. After racing, which takes place from 7.50 p.m. until 10.30 p.m., there is live music and dancing until after midnight.

'It's fabulous to see it packed out, especially by young people who have never been greyhound racing before,' Jim Martin says. 'There are ten races, plus another ten beamed in by satellite from Shelbourne Park in Dublin, and there are no crowd problems.

'Greyhound owners and trainers come from all over the country; we've had the current holder of the Irish greyhound derby race here, and he comes from Co. Tipperary.' The 200-seater restaurant now has to be booked a few months in advance for Friday and Saturday evenings.

It can be anticipated that many of these people will be drawn to the horse racing, so attracting a new and younger market without in any way putting off the diehard racing fans. 'I feel we have come up with something that is unique, from which both sports will benefit,' Jim says. 'The driving force was to safeguard both sports in a businesslike fashion.' One of the safest bets is that this will be achieved. And of those who come initially out of curiosity, many will become regulars.

Horse racing in all its forms, shortly to include all-weather, is an integral part of Irish life and will surely remain so for centuries to come. One name above all others will, I believe, survive down that timespan: Arkle. To have witnessed Arkle in action was one of life's privileges. Everything about him was superlative, from the swinging majesty of his walk (see my Box Brownie camera picture of him walking to the paddock at Sandown) to his flamboyant jumping, from his ability to relax when off duty to his tiger determination to win when the call commanded.

'To grow in stature like Arkle': he would look around him and take in the scene, drawing himself up to his full height, eyes in a calm, steady gaze, ears pricked, body primed for action. Arkle knew he was the best.

And he was.

Arkle, simply the best

INDEX